FRITZ LEIBER

RECOGNITIONS

detective/suspense

Bruce Cassiday, General Editor

Raymond Chandler by Jerry Speir
P. D. James by Norma Siebenheller
John D. MacDonald by David Geherin
Ross Macdonald by Jerry Speir
The Murder Mystique: Crime Writers on Their Art edited by Lucy Freeman
Dorothy L. Sayers by Dawson Gaillard
Sons of Sam Spade: The Private Eye Novel in the 70s by David Geherin

science fiction/fantasy

Sharon Jarvis, General Editor

Isaac Asimov by Jean Fiedler and Jim Mele
Ray Bradbury by Wayne L. Johnson
Critical Encounters: Writers and Themes in Science Fiction edited by Dick Riley
Critical Encounters II: Writers and Themes in Science Fiction edited by Tom Staicar
The Feminine Eye: Science Fiction and the Women Who Write It edited by Tom Staicar
Frank Herbert by Timothy O'Reilly
Ursula K. LeGuin by Barbara J. Bucknall
Theodore Sturgeon by Lucy Menger

Also of Interest

The Bedside, Bathtub & Armchair Companion to Agatha Christie edited by Dick Riley and Pam McAllister
Introduction by Julian Symons

Fritz Leiber

Tom Staicar

Frederick Ungar Publishing Co.
New York

Library of Congress Cataloging in Publication Data
Staicar, Tom.
Fritz Leiber.

(Recognitions)
Bibliography: p.
Includes index.
1. Leiber, Fritz, 1910- —Criticism and interpretation. I. Title. II. Series.
PS3523.E4583Z86 1983 813′.54 83-827
ISBN 0-8044-2836-0
ISBN 0-8044-6875-3 (pbk.)

To my wife, Joy.

CONTENTS

Preface

This is the first full-length book about Fritz Leiber, the only writer yet to have earned both the title of Grand Master from the Science Fiction Writers of America and the World Fantasy Convention's Life Achievement Award. To toil in one area of literature for many years may result in success, but to excel in several different ones sets a writer apart. Only Leiber has covered such a wide range of speculative fiction, having written a disaster novel, a heroic fantasy series, contemporary science fiction, and horror. Unlike the usual Jack-of-all-trades, however, he is a master of them all. He received a Hugo Award for the best novel of the year for *The Big Time*, and later, for *The Wanderer*. He has also won the Nebula Award, the British Fantasy Society's August Derleth Award, and the World Fantasy Award. *Conjure Wife* and *Our Lady of Darkness*, his two modern horror novels, are highly acclaimed. Leiber has won more awards for more types of fiction than any of his peers.

Leiber has written about such diverse characters and backgrounds as a pair of sword-wielding warriors in the ancient city of Lankhmar, a young college professor trapped by witchcraft, and a visitor from a space colony who touches off a revolution in the empire of Texas—to name only a few. Leiber's fancy may take them to far-off times and places, yet humanity remains his first concern, and his human vision one of his greatest strengths.

He anticipated the sociological and psychological science fiction of the present day, being one of the first science-fiction writers to tackle the subject of the human mind in a society bent on crushing individuality. In *The Green Millennium* there is a Federal Bureau of Morality that censors the arts in line with "proper" moral guidelines, and in *A Specter Is Haunting Texas* the president's term is expected to be from "inauguration to assassination." Political satire and commentary crop up repeatedly in his works. A strong exponent of individuality, in *Gather, Darkness!* Leiber explores what happens when church and state merge in a scientific theocracy, while in *Night of the Wolf*, murder has replaced love as a source of excitement.

A pacifist for much of his life, Leiber has spoken out against the insanity of war. In one of his writings, "death notices" have replaced draft notices, and young men must quietly go to die so that others will not have to face actual combat. In another, he traces the final days of Edgar Allan Poe, as the writer's premonitions of the impending Civil War begin to suffocate him.

Leiber, like many other science-fiction writers, is fascinated by time travel. But while traditional science fiction cautions the traveler against disturbing anything for fear of diverting the course of later civilization, Leiber's series of Change War stories takes the opposite tack. In them, time soldiers must counteract the inertia of the Law of Conservation of Time—changes in the past can indeed be snuffed out, canceling the efforts of those who have battled in the ancient world and destroying their adversaries in the future.

In his most acclaimed works, Fritz Leiber writes about the human predicament of being a single person within the context of an enormous, uncaring universe. How these people cope and manage to transcend their difficulties is his real topic, regardless of the horror, fantasy, or science-fiction trappings. He writes about future societies we hope will never exist, and about ones that seem to be coming true with every day's headlines.

This book covers Leiber's entire career and is arranged by subject rather than chronologically. Notes follow the text and are identified by page number and a few words from the relevant passage. A chronology and selected bibliography are included.

Using my extensive personal collection, and with some assistance from the interlibrary loan staffs of research libraries, I have examined all of Leiber's writings. I must here express my gratitude to Fritz Leiber for extending me the courtesy of a lengthy interview, followed by some replies to my questions by mail. His cooperation and encouragement are greatly appreciated. I would also like to thank my wife, Joy, whose valuable comments and suggestions were of much help to me in writing this book.

T.S.

1

Master of All Trades

Fritz Leiber is a tall, slender, distinguished-looking man in his early seventies. Many people have remarked that his speaking voice has a theatrical resonance, enhanced by early training in Shakespearean roles. His dignified appearance and bearing have been characterized as "imposing."

These impressions tell only part of the story. A complex and intelligent man, Leiber is also a warm person. Science-fiction fans have written to him and have then been surprised when he invites them to his apartment for a chat. He somehow finds time to write for small journals as a favor and to speak on panels at fantasy and SF conventions, answering fans' questions.

Leiber's father, Fritz, Sr., born in Chicago in 1910, and his mother, Virginia, were both professional actors based in that city. When not living with relatives, such as his maternal grandmother in Pontiac, Michigan, young Fritz toured with his parents, learning to recite lines from Shakespeare before learning how to read. The travel, the props, the plays, and the general atmosphere of the theater permeated his childhood and later worked themselves into some of his fiction.

He developed a fear of the dark as a child, and later recalled being afraid, after he saw a production of *The Cat and the Canary,* that hands were coming out of the walls. Some of his reading matter gave him anxiety, too; a few of H. P. Lovecraft's horror stories made him uneasy for weeks. Despite this, Leiber read Verne, Wells, and Edgar Rice Burroughs as a teenager. He started reading *Amazing Stories* in its first year (1926) as part of a lifelong devotion to SF.

But as the son of an established actor, Fritz was expected to follow in his father's footsteps. While his father had acted in such silent films as *Cleopatra* (opposite Theda Bara) and had his own repertory company for many years, young Fritz did not choose to become an actor, although he appeared in brief roles. He remembered later that his family had anticipated he would eventually organize his own troupe, creating a family theater dynasty like the Barrymores. At just the time Fritz was ready to earn his own living, the Depression of the 1930s dealt a severe blow to live theater in the United States. Any job in any field of endeavor was difficult to find.

Writing became Fritz's main interest in life after he got the notion to write a story for his favorite magazine, *Weird Tales*. He recalled that his parents had not actively discouraged him from writing:

> I think I never really did rebel against my family. I think that my father and mother were sympathetic to my writing but they made the typical suggestions that *any* sensible person would make: why try so hard to sell stories to *Weird Tales* when *The Saturday Evening Post* pays so much more? That was just *sound* in its way.

The jobs at which Fritz worked while learning his craft were his main sources of income. To earn one's living by writing alone has always been difficult, and Leiber started out in an era when magazines paid poorly, paperbacks did not exist, no television or film rights went to writers of science fiction or fantasy, works which rarely saw print in book form. Fritz was not to become a full-time writer until 1956.

He attended the University of Chicago and earned a Bachelor of Philosophy degree in 1932. In 1933, after placing a few children's stories in *The Churchman*, he was persuaded to enter the General Theological Seminary in New York City. He then became lay reader and minister at various Episcopal churches in New Jersey that had lacked full-time ministers. After some five months he grew dissatisfied with this life and left the ministry, returning to the University of Chicago with the intention of completing a master's degree in philosophy.

While attending classes there he met English-born Jonquil Stephens, another aspiring writer. They were married in 1936. Fritz worked for a publisher in Chicago, editing and revising material for *The Standard American Encyclopedia* and *The University of*

Knowledge. Their son, Justin, was born in 1938. (As an adult Justin was to earn a Ph.D. in philosophy and himself establish an academic career as well as one in writing. *Beyond Rejection* (1980) is a science-fiction first novel about the transfer of a dead man's consciousness into a young woman's body.)

A friend Leiber had met at the University of Chicago, named Harry Otto Fischer, was another would-be writer, and the two began a relationship based mostly upon their voluminous letters through the years. Although Fischer did not pursue a writing career, he did supply some important ideas and fragments of stories which formed the basis of Leiber's heroic fantasy series about Fafhrd and the Gray Mouser.

Using Fischer's idea about the nature of the two characters, Leiber wrote the story "Two Sought Adventure." It sold (and would later become part of the saga that grew to six volumes, revised as "Lords of Quarmall"). He made the sum of $125.00, based on a rate of one cent per word. Since he was earning only $25.00 per week at his regular nine-to-five job, he decided he would quit and use the time to dash off one 12,000-word tale each month. Unfortunately, his second sale was made one year later.

A freelance writing career set aside for the time being, he took up other jobs, including teaching speech and drama at Occidental College in Los Angeles. During the early 1940s, he continued to write and submit fiction.

His writing began to gain recognition as he sold stories to the prestigious magazines *Unknown* and *Astounding*, both guided by the premier science-fiction editor of the era, John W. Campbell, Jr. Supernatural horror stories, heroic fantasy tales, and straight science-fiction stories began to flow from Leiber's typewriter.

World War II hit the pacifist Leiber hard. Still wrestling with his antiwar beliefs, he took a job as a precision inspector at the Douglas Aircraft Company in Santa Monica, California, doing defense work. Partly to avoid his being drafted, the act also symbolized Leiber's growing understanding that, as he would later conclude, all wars may be a waste of human lives but World War II was justified because of the horrors brought by Hitler and the Nazis. Pacifism and the struggle of conscience over such matters became a major influence in his writings.

Working at jobs such as assistant editor, and later, associate editor, for the magazine *Science Digest* (1944–1956), Leiber pursued his fiction-writing career as a part-time occupation. He researched and wrote articles on science topics that appeared in the magazine, and at the same time wrote novels and stories. The growing audience for his works allowed him to become a full-time writer after 1956.

2

The Biting Edge: Satire

The Silver Eggheads was first published as a short novel in *The Magazine of Fantasy and Science Fiction* in 1958 and was expanded to book length in 1961. The novel is Leiber's longest humorous fiction. In it he manages to satirize the entire publishing scene, as well as to comment upon American contemporary society and the uses to which it puts advanced technology.

In a future America, writers are caretakers of a form of computer system called wordmills. Wordmills turn out fictional works of all types, after being fed information about market conditions, reader demographic profiles, and a brief description of the kind of book desired. (Little wordmills write children's books.) Paperbacks produce sounds, smells, and tactile sensations, which enter the minds of the readers through suggestion. The success of wordmill books has created a strong demand for more of the same product, manufactured mostly along Readership Row in New Angeles, California.

Gaspard de la Nuit is an example of an evolved future writer, living a life of ease thanks to the advent of the wordmills: "He had spent his graveyard shift dozing, drinking coffee, and finishing reading *Sinners of the Satellite Suburbs* and *Everyman His Own Philosopher.* An author really couldn't ask for an easier night's writing."

Gaspard is a journeyman writer, but looks forward to becoming a licensed master writer. As such, he will no longer have to wear an elaborate costume and smoke a meerschaum pipe; he will be "licensed to wear Levis and sweatshirt, get a crewcut, and smoke cigarettes in public." In contrast, journeyman writers must keep up appearances for their public, and this usually entails wearing doublet and hose, a Roman toga, or a complete Cyrano de Bergerac costume. The public demands atmosphere from its writers, and this is the hardest part of the occupation, since the actual writing is done by the wordmills.

The jacket copy on one of Gaspard de la Nuit's novels gives the following apocryphal account of his background:

> Gaspard de la Nuit is a French dishwasher who has had extracurricular experience as a spaceship steward, abortionist's helper (working undercover to collect evidence for the Sûreté), Montmartre taxidriver, valet to a *vicomte* of the *ancien régime*, high-topper in the pine forests of French Canada, student of interplanetary law at the Sorbonne, Huguenot missionary to the black Martians, and piano player in a *maison de joie*.

Unlike most of his peers, Gaspard likes to read books, "especially the near-hypnotic wordmill product, sometimes called wordwooze, with its warm rosy clouds of adjectives, its action verbs like wild winds blowing, its four-dimensionally solid nouns and electrowelded connectives." The jacket copy mentions that "he wrote his latest bestseller *Passwords to Passion* in two and one-third days on a brand-new Pocket Wordmaster equipped with Floating Adverbs and Five-Second Suspense Injection. He polished the novel on a Simon Super-juicer."

Gaspard is in love with fellow writer Heloise Ibsen. Their relationship was at first partly inspired by publicity demands, although the two then fell truly in love. But because of his fraternization with robots, Heloise has called him "a dirty robot-lover." *The Silver Eggheads* portrays robots metaphorically as blacks or other minorities, similar to the use of robots in the Asimov robot stories. Part of the subplot of *The Silver Eggheads* deals with the robots' yearning for respect and rights, and the humans' resentment at losing their security and livelihoods to them—as the humans perceive the situation. Leiber sides with the robots. He shows robots as psychiatrists, electricians, and teachers with problems and needs.

According to "Saint Isaac" (Isaac Asimov, whose Laws of Robotics have influenced nearly every writer in SF), robots aren't supposed to harm human beings. The robots in *The Silver Eggheads* have developed human-style sensitivity, such as female robots' modesty about having their electrical sockets open to public view. A necessary jolt from batteries must be given only in private, so that others will not consider it a vulgar act.

The main plot of the novel concerns a revolt of the writers, who demand that they be released from the tyranny of wordmill tending. They are led by radicals such as Homer Hemingway, who has sabotaged a newsstand and left a banner with "30" across it in black.* Under the slogan "Smash Wordmills" they set out to end "mill-swill" and return to their rightful roles as true writers. They speculate about the old days—which they never actually knew—and about how different it must have been to assemble a book word by word, "like building pyramids." Rather than having a wordmill to feed a general pattern and then wait for it to pick the right words to fit a formula, the earlier writers could deviate from the simple story if they wished.

The revolt reaches every wordmill as sabotage increases:

> Homer Hemingway axed through the sedate gray control panel of a Random House Write-All and went fiercely to work on the tubes and transistors. Sappho Wollstonecraft Shaw shoved a large plastic funnel into the memory unit of a Scribner Scribe and poured two gallons of smoking nitric acid into its indescribably delicate innards. . . .
>
> Agatha Ngaio Sayers poisoned a Doubleday 'Dunnit with powdered magnetic oxide. Somerset Makepeace Dickens sledgehammered a Harcourt Hack. H. G. Heinlein planted stiletto explosives in an Appleton S-F and almost lost his life pushing the rest of the mob back to a safe distance until the fiery white jets had stabbed through the involuted leagues of fine silver wiring. . . . Fritz Ashton Eddison loosed a cloud of radioactive bats inside a Fiction House Fantasizer (really a rebuilt Dutton Dreamer with Fingertip Credibility Control). . . .

We see that Leiber satirized his own name in combination with fantasy writers Clark Ashton Smith and E. R. Eddison to create Fritz Ashton Eddison. Use of such combinations as Edgar Allan Bloch

* The symbol "30" was once used in the typesetting of newspapers to indicate "the end" of an article.

and Conan Haggard de Camp heighten the comic effect of the mob scene.

Although the publishers call out robot goons to stop the writers, the revolt is a success and the Readership Row wordmills are completely destroyed, thus eliminating the only source of mechanized writing in the English-speaking solar system. The public is outraged. There is a run on the bookstores, whose product has to be rationed.

Shortly after the wordmills are gone, the writers set to work. Unfortunately, they quickly discover that they cannot write. Decades of laziness have created an entire generation of so-called writers who cannot set words on paper. Despite "tankcars of coffee," there seems to be no inspiration forthcoming. Recreating the life-styles of earlier writers in garrets, they decide they should "kick ideas around." They viewed the earlier practice of writing as "a kind of alcoholic parlor football with bedroom rest periods, terminated by miracles."

The frustrations of the writers who now find themselves afflicted with king-size writer's blocks leads to desperate measures, none of them effective. Looking back, they decide that twentieth-century writers must have been hacks of some sort who had editors to write outlines for them and then simply filled in the words. When society became too complex for any single writer to understand or write about, the computers began augmenting their efforts. Market pressures on the publishers, and the writers' neuroses and demands for big royalties, caused the publishers to rely more upon the computers:

> Naturally a machine that could be owned and kept in one place would be incomparably more efficient than a stable of writers galloping around, changing publishers, organizing unions and guilds, demanding higher royalties, having psychoses and sports cars and mistresses and neurotic children, exploding their temperaments all over the lot, and even trying to sneak weird notions of their own into editor-perfected stories.

Since robots do not indulge in such behavior, one might suppose they could provide a solution to the dearth of fiction, but this is not the case. Zane Gort (named after the robot in the SF film *The Day the Earth Stood Still* and the Western writer Zane Grey) is an example of a robot who tries to write, but he is willing only to turn out stories about robots, for robot readers. His ambition is to help humans and robots work more closely together and to get humans to like robots. He is willing to coauthor a book with his friend Gaspard, but the project does not bear fruit. Aside from Zane Gort, other robots do not seem to be interested in producing any fiction.

Nearly forgotten are another possible literary source, the "silver eggheads," a group of human brains preserved for two hundred years after the deaths of their bodies, and so named because they were enclosed in egg-shaped silver cases on pedestals. Robotics expert Daniel Zukertort developed a mind-to-metal synapse which allowed brains to be preserved and yet still function. Although the application of this theory might have been to produce prosthetic bodies for the brains, Zukertort used it only to preserve the greatest minds of mankind. Blood is recycled by a pump and a filtering mechanism, and connections provide nutrients to the brains.

When Zukertort dies, he leaves no notes behind. When the story about thirty preserved writers' brains reaches the public, they demand immortality for their own brains. They fear that the eggheads will prove malevolent and resent that the method of preserving brains is now lost forever. But once convinced that the eggheads are actually helpless, childlike, paralyzed entities that can not move out of their laboratory setting, the public gradually forgets about them. Although it is known that the thinkers were important, their names are not on record any longer; the brains decided years earlier to become anonymous men and women. There is speculation that such writers as Theodore Sturgeon might be among them.

The life of a brain detached forever from its body might be either a blessing or a curse. No pain or bodily needs or aging would be experienced, but neither would physical pleasure or freedom of movement. Terrifying boredom and possible madness might result. Science-fiction writers have considered such situations from both sides, as they have with immortality (either an exciting chance to explore the world, or an agonizingly boring situation that repetition renders meaningless).

In *The Silver Eggheads,* the brains are now attended by Nurse Bishop, who has named one Rusty, another Half-Pint, and so on, because of the external characteristics of their shells. Special speakers have been attached, allowing them to sing, sigh, or make "free noises," but the keepers of the eggheads permit this only on weekends and holidays. Another rule for "the nursery"—the demeaning term for the eggheads' home—is that no wordwooze can be read to them.

The eggheads become uninterested in the affairs of mankind, choosing to be totally withdrawn, thinking about the creation or destruction of worlds. One egghead tells Nurse Bishop that he once read an H. P. Lovecraft story "The Whisperer in Darkness," in which aliens from Pluto put men's brains in metal cylinders, and these brains become estranged from the rest of mankind. (The Lovecraft story was obviously an influence on Leiber.)

The rest of the novel chronicles the writers' and publishers' attempts to get the eggheads to write, and of the robots' and antirobot forces' efforts to get along. These two plots provide satirical ammunition for Leiber. Robots praise the fiction of "Saint Isaac" and "Saint Eando"; robots have their literary gurus also. (The names refer to Isaac Asimov and Earl and Otto Binder, who, as Eando Binder, wrote robot stories.) And freelance writing is not dead. A publisher remarks that the slushpile (the unsolicited manuscripts stack) is still full, although no submissions from nonwordmill sources have been sought for over one hundred years.

The novel leaves the future open to more creations by people rather than machines, on the theory that the audience will learn how to grapple with real ideas even though they have enjoyed being lulled for generations by wordwooze, the hypnotically manipulative wordmill books. An interactive relationship between man and robot, and between man and machine, is also a possibility.

Leiber uses satire in several ways. The robots exhibit many of the problems that black Americans have had within the larger society of white people. When Zane Gort and the other robots have had contacts with humans, the relationships always differed from those between humans, or from those of robots with robots. The segregation of and bias toward robots mirrors that of whites toward blacks, especially before the civil rights legislation passed several years after *The Silver Eggheads* was published. The idea of robots writing only for robots is similar to black writers who have decided to write only about the black experience, feeling that black pride was more important than the acceptance afforded through assimilation into the white culture. In the 1960s this separateness became a source of the slogan "black is beautiful," moving away from the earlier trend toward blending into the larger culture.

While satirizing editors and publishers and their relationships with writers, Leiber also anticipated the trend toward computerization of all aspects of publishing. Writers have begun using word processors, computers that generate manuscripts and allow for alterations in words or format. The writer uses a computer keyboard in place of a typewriter and can create a computer tape of the manuscript while watching a cathode-ray tube similar to a television screen. As of the early 1980s, word processors could aid writers in editing their work and in producing the printout copy of the writing in corrected form with proper margins. The wordmills in Leiber's novel are far in advance of the state of the art in word processors today.

It is true, however, that other aspects of publishing reflect the trend toward computerization. The setting of books into type, accounting and billing, the shipping of books to retailers, and the purchase of books by local bookstores are all handled by computers, at least in the larger publishing houses. Large bookselling chains keep close track of sales in all their local bookstores by computers that count each sale. Leiber anticipated this use of computers in a general sense.

Extrapolating from what some observers contend are the current teaching trends, this future America has writers who are illiterate or semiliterate. Continuing the trends of the 1950s and 1960s toward new teaching methods that deviated from the basics, reading and writing have been deemphasized. In Leiber's novel, voicewriters can translate words directly into print. Spoken language need not progress further than "Simplified Basic" or "Solar Pidgin."

Here Leiber is satirizing liberal teaching styles and increased use of audiovisual aids, learning through television, and learning by listening, which Marshall McLuhan discussed in his books. In *Understanding Media* (1964) and *The Medium Is the Message* (1967) McLuhan discussed the implications for a society that depended upon TV for its political news, TV and radio for its fictional characters, and the spoken word transmitted electronically for its communications. Generations brought up to learn by listening since the advent of TV and radio were thought less likely to become literate adults. *The Silver Eggheads* satirizes such trends through absurd exaggeration.

Through improbable farce, *The Silver Eggheads* punctures the inflated self-images of writers, editors, and publishers. The novel succeeds as humor and also as a vehicle for satire. It is similar to those of science-fiction writer Ron Goulart in that they combine slapstick, parody, and humorous caricature. (Goulart also features robots in several novels.) But within the context of Leiber's body of work, *The Silver Eggheads* is a relatively minor book. It is significant in its attempt at humor—quite rare in science fiction. Aside from some fantasy novels, there are few humorous science-fiction novels, possibly because suspension of disbelief, so important to the genre, requires plausible backgrounds, while humor always points out the ridiculous, the illogical.

The 1953 science-fiction novel *The Green Millennium* centers around a young man named Phil Gish, whose life is changed forever by the sudden appearance of a green cat on his windowsill. Up to its arrival, his romantic life has been a failure, his relationship with his parents has been unhappy, and education has always seemed to end for him with "signs saying 'restricted' or 'subversive' or the even more maddening blank signs of calculated silence. . ." Phil Gish is also upset because robots have taken his job, although they offer no competition in the occupation of combat soldier.

But just as the cat arrives, Phil's mood turns happy, and he feels better about life. Naming the cat Lucky, he finds the appearance of any cat to be unusual, since cats and dogs were slaughtered as possible germ carriers during biological warfare epidemics.

Gish finds himself involved with one complication after another, most of them due to his string of oddball acquaintances. The future America in *The Green Millennium* is one with a Federal Bureau of Loyalty and a Federal Bureau of Morality, each with scores of agents observing the citizens, and armed with lasers and heat-sensitive missiles. When an organized crime syndicate finds out that Phil has the green cat, it competes fiercely against government agents to locate Lucky.

Dr. Romadka, a psychiatrist, tells Phil that America itself is going through an age of madness:

> Not that this current social madness is a deep secret or anything to be startled at. What other results could have been expected when American society began to overvalue on the one hand security, censorship, an imagined world-saving idealism and self-sacrifice in war, and on the other hand an insatiable hunger for possessions, fiercely competitive aggressiveness, sadistic male belligerence, contempt for parents and the state, and a fantastically overstimulated sexuality?

Leiber is pointing out that the stress in the urban American lifestyle causes fads, symptoms of aggressiveness, and even madness. As an example, the hypocritical religious leader turned politician, President Robert T. Barnes, is secretly allied with the conglomerate Fun, Incorporated, a chain of entertainment arcades and amusement centers, one of which is the All Pleasures Park. "Handies" (radio-operated electronic devices which offer sexual stimulation in place of human contact) are available for purchase, as are admission to male-female wrestling and jukebox burlesque. All this bears out Dr. Romadka's opinions about America.

Phil thinks he sees a young woman through the apartment window across from his who takes off her shoes to reveal horse's hooves. This brings him to Dr. Romadka, and the psychiatrist tells him this episode was merely a delusion brought on by stress, possibly a sexual delusion because it may link sex in Phil's mind with a punishing and trampling animal—the horse—in the manner that ancient myths told of nymphs and satyrs. He believes that, unconsciously, Phil wants to be taught about love.

Significantly the psychiatrist mentions the story of Pandora. "She was not an ordinary girl sent by the gods to bring mankind a box containing all ills. No, she was a metal maiden, forged by Hephaestus at the command of Zeus. In other words, an automaton, a robot—bringing in this case the ills of the Second Industrial Revolution caused by the introduction of electronic calculators and sensers." The great panic in Atom War Two brought out neurotic delusions in many people, and the doctor believes Phil suffers from them. The two atomic wars have destroyed America's social structure, and in an effort to maintain control, the government has resorted to widespread surveillance of private citizens.

Phil fears he might be overheard by someone who will turn him in to the Federal Bureau of Loyalty. "Psychologists, he supposed, knew things that were never told to ordinary people: seemingly innocent symbols that stamped men as cowards, rapists, murderers, traitors, crypto-communists, non-conformists." Phil could end up in a mental institution if someone like Dr. Romadka decided to consign him to one, and this could mean torture therapy.

With the help of the doctor's daughter, Mitzie, he escapes from the office. But once the true nature of Lucky is uncovered, Federal agents suspect Phil and the cat of subversive activities. The cat can project happy or fearful moods by its presence. At one point, a row of guards gives up their resistance and lets Phil pass by, because Lucky suddenly turned them into complacent, contented people. The Federal Bureau of Loyalty places a top priority on capturing Lucky, whom they believe must have been bred specially by the Russians. This is because of Russian experiments to raise animals with extrasensory perception.

Both Dr. Romadka and the government agents have reasonable hunches. Lucky is no ordinary cat, and love—or symbols of it—is entering Phil's life. He meets Dora Pannes (a slightly altered anagram of "Pandora"), a violet-haired woman he likes, although he learns eventually that she is a robot. The woman with hooves, Dytie da Silva, turns out to be a space alien, and her hooves are real. Her first name is short for Aphrodite, the goddess of love. Like Lucky, she is part of an invasion force of two types of aliens, who most resemble house cats and satyrs, and who have developed a symbiotic relationship. The invasion is intended to bring about a peaceful revolution promoting love and brotherhood on Earth, to save the planet from decline and eventual destruction.

Lucky is from the eighth planet of the star Vega. Like a pet who brings harmony into a home, Lucky and his fellow aliens can bring harmony to Earth by projecting hormones into the air around them, greatly affecting people's emotions. Having monitored Earth broadcasts and learned how to better disguise themselves in order to infiltrate the populations of Earth, they arrived in a ship which was rendered invisible.

The novel reflects the author's political ideas, especially his anti-McCarthyism. Senator Joseph McCarthy and his followers grabbed headlines by searching out Communists and "fellow-travelers"—alledged Communist sympathizers—among public figures following World War II. At the peak of his power, McCarthy's mere mention of a certain official's possible link with a Communist ruined that person's career. Most opinion now holds that this was a witch hunt built on generally groundless accusations, attacks on people through guilt by association more often than on substantive evidence, the accusers chiefly motivated by the desire for political power. The epithet "McCarthy tactics" was used against politicians in the 1960s and '70s who tried to discredit enemies in a similar manner. Blacklisting of actors or writers because of petitions they signed or their political affiliations is sometimes said to be "McCarthyist." In the early 1950s, liberal and left-wing thinkers lived in fear of losing their livelihoods if McCarthy or his supporters decided to single them out.

Leiber not only parodies the witch hunts of the early 1950s, he satirizes what he saw in American life-styles that helped bring about this political persecution—too high a value placed on security and material goods. In establishing Phil Gish as a sympathetic character and having him endangered by a repressive government, Leiber declares his belief in individual freedom.

Some of the fears about the future that Leiber expressed in the early 1950s have come true today. Phil resented losing his job to robots, in this case the mechanical mail sorters that replaced people at the post office. Such sorters actually did replace people who had worked in some phases of mail handling in the 1970s. The idea of technological innovations causing loss of jobs was a topic of some discussion when Leiber wrote about it, but it has become an important part of the employment picture in the United States in the 1980s. Computers and robots of various types are superseding people who used to do a variety of jobs, from automobile production welding through hundreds of office tasks, such as the handling of invoices and records.

A housing shortage alluded to at one point in the novel was said to be in the 1980s. This came true, due to soaring interest rates, labor costs, and inflation. New housing is in very short supply.

The Moral Majority movement seems somewhat similar to a Federal Bureau of Morality, although there are differences between the two. The Moral Majority is a private group that opposes what it sees as immoral practices through political lobbying. The fictional Federal Bureau of Morality was a government group, with tactics much different from the Moral Majority, but it opposed immorality among the citizens.

The male-female wrestling mentioned was not such a far-fetched idea, as it turns out. Although corporate involvement has not yet happened, female mud wrestling is an entertainment found in urban areas in the 1980s. A few instances of simulated male-female mud wrestling are even on record, including a Cheryl Ladd special aired on network television in 1979. In the 1950s such a practice might have sounded science-fictional, but this lurid form of entertainment has a certain following.

The violence taken for granted in *The Green Millennium* is becoming more common as the decades pass. The Jim Jones cult, the Charles Manson family murders, a number of attempted and carried-out political murders, and the type of violence sometimes perpetrated by punk rock stars would fit easily within the context of Leiber's fictional America. Even antipersonnel bombs and individual laser weapons similar to Leiber's are being refined today for use by terrorists and antiterrorist squads.

The platform shoes worn by women in the novel were an actual fashion trend during the 1970s. The All Pleasures Amusement Park does not exist, unless we lump together theme amusement parks, video game arcades, massage parlors, and other modes of entertainment available today.

The Soviets continue to experiment with ESP. There is also a similarity between Dr. Romadka's incorrect accusation that the United States was attempting to make broadcasts against the Soviets by means of specially-bred green cats, and the real-life Soviet use of microwaves. As reported in many journals, the Soviets repeatedly attempted to harm American diplomats in Moscow by beaming microwave pulsations at them. Experiments with laboratory animals have shown, on a limited basis, that the waves can control heartbeats to the point of bringing on seizures and can cause sexual impotence and mental confusion.

The time-honored science-fictional elements of alien invasion, exaggeration of current trends, and the viewing of American customs through alien eyes were all used by Leiber. He manages to make quite a few statements about American life as well as some predictions which, coincidentally, have come true.

The Green Millennium has gone through several paperback editions and continues to appeal to readers who enjoy lighthearted SF. ("Poor Superman" and "Coming Attraction," two stories set in the same future America, were reprinted in *The Best of Fritz Leiber* in 1974.)

A Specter Is Haunting Texas was Leiber's satirical comment on the America of the Vietnam war era, especially of President Lyndon B. Johnson's administration. Leiber had been active in the Johnson campaign against Barry Goldwater in 1964, and he was bitterly disappointed when Johnson's election did not bring an end to the war. Feeling betrayed by the Democratic president, Leiber wrote *A Specter Is Haunting Texas* to deflate the pomposity and egotism he saw in Johnson's Texan associates.

The novel's title paraphrases the opening of *The Communist Manifesto:* "A specter is haunting Europe, the specter of Communism." Leiber's tale begins with an imaginary quotation about the history of Texas from a book written by a black underground movement leader who lives in Watts-Angeles. Part of the excerpt reads:

> Ever since Lyndon ousted Jack in the Early Atomic Age, the term of a President of Texas has been from inauguration to assassination. Murder is merely the continuation of politics by other means. Power ennobles, but Petroleum Power ennobles absolutely. The end of life is liberty. Texans are empowered to enjoy, exploit, and handle liberty, while Mexes, Unjuns, and Nigras—all those having dark faces or a dark hole in their pocketbooks—have the privilege of serving liberty and keeping their hands off it.

That quotation sets the tone for the novel, which criticizes Texans for cruelty, as seen through the eyes of Scully, a newly arrived visitor from the orbiting space colony Circumluna. Circumluna, once a research colony circling the Earth, was first a self-sustaining colony that supported a population of hundreds, and later, revolted and won independence. Scully's full name is Scully Christopher Crockett La Cruz, and he has lived all his life in the zero-gravity conditions of space. He is eight feet eight inches tall, weighs 147 pounds with his metal exoskeleton on, and 97 pounds without it. He wears the titanium suit to keep his extremely thin and weak body from being crushed by Earth's gravity. In space, his bones and muscles developed in deficient form because they had no gravity to push against. His exoskeleton electronically transmits the slightest motions of his body in any direction, allowing full, robotlike movements.

Scully's awakening on Earth is filled with surprises. His shuttle ship, the *Tsiolkovsky* (named after the Russian SF writer), did not end up in Canada as he had planned. He is in "Dallas, Texas, Texas—the heart of the human universe and the golden laurel crown of her culture." Elmo, an Earth dweller who greets him, tells him that many changes have taken place since contact with the orbiting Circumluna colony broke down:

> Scully, son, ever since the Great Texasward Industrial Migration and World War Three, Texas has extended from the Nicaraguan Canal to the North Pole, including most of Central America, all of Mexico, nearly all of Canada, and all that matters of the Fibbertygibbet Forty-seven—I mean the former United States of America. That is, at present. We Texans might take a fancy to extend our boundaries any day. There's Cuba to be reconquered, and Indochina, and Ireland, and Hawaii, and Hither Siberia. But on the whole, we Texans are a shoot-and-let-shoot people. We whipped the Cherokees and the Mexicans and we tied the Russians and Chinese, and we're inclined to rest on our laurels—unless, of course, roused, when we get dynamic as an automated cottonpicking rig goosed by the program for an Irish jig.

The white people of Texas are allowed to take growth-inducing hormones and thus grow to seven or eight feet tall. Some get to be twelve feet in height, but die young from the strain on their internal organs. (Scully is only accepted by the Texans because of his height, even though they question his off-Earth upbringing.) Blacks not already eliminated by past wars or riots now live in small enclaves such as Watts-Angeles. Mexicans are slavelike second-class citizens given hormones that keep them short and hunchbacked, as if to symbolize their lower status among the whites.

Upon his arrival, the Mexicans immediately begin calling Scully "El Espectro" (the Specter) because his appearance suggests that of the Specter, a character in ancient legend who will supposedly arrive someday to free the Mexicans by leading a revolution. Scully shares with the Specter a lanky, emaciated body and a black robe with hood, and in time, the Mexicans come to believe that Scully actually is the messianic Specter. They become inspired to demand more rights and to organize for revolution.

As an outsider being shown around Texas, Scully is told about the superior manner in which white Texans live:

> You see, Scully, a man can't feel really free unless he's got a lot of underfolk to boss around. That's one of the great paradoxes of liberty, first discovered by those proto-Texans, the ancient Greeks, who had slaves to burn, though I don't think they actually burned them much until Nero's day, or maybe the discovery of gasoline, which permitted Deep South lynching bees and Buddhist immolations alike.

The latter reference is to the mid-1960s protests against the Vietnam war by Southeast Asian monks, who set themselves on fire in order to attract sympathy for the antiwar movement. *Life, Time, Newsweek,* and other magazines featured stories on the Buddhist immolations shortly before Leiber began writing his novel.

Scully is quickly attracted to a young woman he meets, who goes under the name La Cucaracha. She tells him about the development of the Mexican culture in Texas after World War III. Despite these advances, many Mexicans must wear yokes that transmit information and impulses into their bodies, controlling their work and movements. At night these can be removed, allowing a few brief hours of relative freedom after a hard day of labor.

History is distorted by the Texans, who maintain that the list of their prominent citizens includes Leif Ericson, Paul Bunyan, Big Bill Thompson, John L. Sullivan, William Randolph Hearst, and Abraham Lincoln. Since 1845, the Texans believe, Texas was secretly the true head of the United States and even ran both sides during the Civil War. Presidents were just figureheads for the leadership which actually resided in Texas. Texan Jack Garner secretly bossed Franklin D. Roosevelt, and Lyndon B. Johnson bossed John F. Kennedy. Kennedy was posthumously declared an honorary Texan "because of the grandeur and ritual importance of his demise." After World War III, with Washington and other major cities destroyed, the power of Texas could be revealed to the public, and Texans openly took the helm of government.

At one point Elmo mentions that California has been mostly black since the assassination of "Ronald the Third." This is apparently a reference to Ronald Reagan, then Governor of California, when massive riots by blacks destroyed millions of dollars of property and brought police crackdowns in the late 1960s.

Like Leiber, Scully is an actor. He played roles in his own repertory company in the La Cruz Theater in the Sphere (rather than Theater in the Round), having appeared as Tom Sawyer, Jommy Cross (from the van Vogt classic *Slan*), and in other roles. Tom Sawyer was notable for his independence and, in the science-fiction novel *Slan*, Jommy Cross is a mutant superior to the majority of the population but nonetheless a hunted outcast. Both of these characters are similar to Scully.

The real reason Scully came to Earth was to journey to Yellowknife, Saskatchewan, Canada, to make a mining claim and return with enough money to save his people from deportation from Circumluna. Anyone not doing useful work for the "Longhairs" (the anti-Earth Circumlunans) risks deportation, but a sufficient bribe might stop this practice. Scully has been told that a long-lost pitchblende mine belongs to him, located in Yellowknife and once owned by Aleutians, who bought it from a Cree Indian.

The story is complicated by the fact that a Texan woman, Rachel Vachel, has fallen madly in love with Scully. Governor Lamar, her father, is using Scully as bait in an effort to draw out the Mexican sympathizers and destroy the rebellion. Her rival for Scully, La Cucaracha, is working for the revolution. Several daring escapes take place, but Scully is finally caught.

Tied down and taken out of his precious metal exoskeleton, Scully is bludgeoned with rubber torture hoses and then left alone near a swimming pool. Although all his regular "ghost muscles" have atrophied, his fingers and hands are strong. He is able to crawl slowly to the pool. Once he falls into the water, he is again in a weightless condition similar to that in space, and is temporarily safe.

The rest of the novel deals with the revolutionary activities against the imperialistic government, which reflects Leiber's stand against the American involvement in the Vietnam war. He sums up his viewpoint by writing:

> It had been an ideal country for men with grand imaginations, for geographical and industrial pioneers, until they turned the grandeur to grandiosity and began to broadcast it over the newly discovered mass media. We grieved at that robust and shrewd land's fatal weakness for making right, then wrong decisions, and standing by the latter beyond all reason and with puritanic perversity. . . .
>
> A nation that sought to create, simultaneously, in the same people, a glutton's greed for food, comfort, and possessions—and a puritanic morality. Merciless competition—and docile cooperation. Timid safety-mindedness—and reckless self-sacrifice. A hard-boiled but docile young. Worship of success so long as it could be thought due to luck—and hatred of outstandingness granted by nature and/or hard work. Great scientists and scholars—and a contempt for same. The welfare state—and entrenched wealth. The brotherhood of man—and racial discrimination. In short, nul program. Order, counterorder, disorder. No wonder even Texas made more sense than that.

One of the major criticisms against Lyndon B. Johnson during the Vietnam war was his stubbornness about changing his mind once he had made it up. This led, say some critics, to his determination to see the Southeast Asia war through to its conclusion rather than withdraw troops and face charges of being indecisive. Although polls showed changes in the attitudes of many Americans about continuing United States troop involvement beyond 1967, Johnson continued his firm policy in the face of opposition, even within his own political party. The protests against his Vietnam policies helped convince him not to seek reelection. This seems to be the prime example of America's "fatal weakness for making right, then wrong decisions, and standing by the latter beyond all reason and with puritanic perversity."

The disorder that Leiber saw in American society was apparent during the late 1960s. Families and communities were split over whether to favor the soldiers fighting in Vietnam, with patriotic rallies and the display of American flags as expressions of their support, or to fervently oppose sending any more young men there. News reports sometimes likened the urban riots of blacks and the severe strains between generations in American families to the confrontation of North against South in the Civil War. Although the only domestic bloodshed came from violent battles between "hardhats" (prowar construction workers) and antiwar protestors, or between police (or National Guard troops) and either group, Americans were turning against other Americans who did not share their views on the war.

Leiber's use of the exaggerated stereotypes of Texans to satirize America's embracing of Lyndon B. Johnson's personality and policies was particularly biting. That he began the novel with a quotation about a future Texas where one could expect political assassination instead of free elections showed he was writing a novel in which no holds would be barred.

Political murder, race riots, and the power of the military to keep America involved in the unpopular Vietnam war through the entire 1960s motivated Leiber to write his satire. His sympathies lay with the blacks, whose hopelessness was reflected in the Watts riots; with the Vietnamese, whose country was overrun by Communists and Americans; and with those whose power was usurped by military and government leaders regardless of election results. While the perspective gained during the 1970s has affected the way Americans tend to perceive the 1960s, Leiber's book was first published in that earlier decade, and reflects the antiwar, anti-Johnson feelings of liberals of the late 1960s.

In the 1980s it is difficult to visualize the political environment of that period, when hundreds of thousands demonstrated against the war and often against Johnson himself, with chants such as "Hey, hey, LBJ, how many kids did you kill today?" while smaller crowds demonstrated with chants of "Bomb Hanoi" and "America, love it or leave it." Universities were sometimes shut down by riots, and an entire nation was politically divided. It was during this time that Leiber's strong dose of sarcasm formed *A Specter Is Haunting Texas*. Only a handful of SF writers back then chose to deal with current political issues; others included Harlan Ellison, Thomas Disch, and Norman Spinrad.

The world of the average science-fiction writer often reflects a tone of isolation, the so-called science-fiction ghetto. Many SF writers feel as though they are cut off from mainstream writers; their work is separate, their fans are different (and do not read much non-SF), and the critics who examine their works are writing in specialized magazines. Most SF writers decided not to address the political turmoil going on in America in the late 1960s, and some, like Poul Anderson, did not agree with the antiwar sentiments being expressed. Leiber joined the small minority who wrote antiwar stories using SF as the vehicle for satire or allegory.

Oddly enough, some of this novel has come true. "Petroleum Power" became far more important than it was in the 1960s. It had made Texas millionaires wealthy, but it would later make Arab oil producers even wealthier, and "Petroleum Power" would gain political strength during the energy crisis beginning in 1973. The television show "Dallas" became the highest-rated show for many weeks in 1980 and 1981 in most cities. The Texas look in fashion, including cowboy boots, vests, belts, and hats which emulated Western styles, became a popular fashion among young people. Texas-style bars replaced discos in some cities, with mechanical bull riding as a pastime.

One of the most accurate of Leiber's inadvertent predictions was that of the Texasward migration. Due to automobile industry layoffs and the economic slump which followed them, millions of workers in the Midwest and Northeast began looking at the want ads from Texas newspapers, some of which had three-inch-thick sections. The migration of people and industries to Texas, along with other Sun Belt states, established itself as a major trend by 1980.

3

Freedom, Nonconformity, and Alienation

The Sinful Ones, an SF novel that deals with bizarre aspects of life's routines, was originally planned as a short work for magazine publication. Leiber began it in January, 1943, following the publication of his first two novels, *Conjure Wife* and *Gather, Darkness!*, in the magazines *Unknown* and *Astounding*, respectively. He recalls being an otherwise unemployed writer at the time, worried about the draft.

He wrote the first four chapters and mailed them to John W. Campbell, Jr. the influential editor of *Unknown*. The reply came that the World War II paper shortage had forced the magazine to cease publication, and Campbell would no longer be buying any fantasy or supernatural stories. He would buy hard science fiction for *Astounding* only. This meant, at that time, that there was no market for *The Sinful Ones*. Discouraged, Leiber set the project aside and took a job as precision inspector at a defense plant run by Douglas Aircraft in Santa Monica, California.

At the end of World War II, he showed the four sample chapters to a friend, who suggested he try to market the novel. Book publication in the fields of fantasy or SF was nearly nonexistent in the 1940s. Today, a novel might sell to a magazine, a hardcover publisher, a paperback publisher, possibly a film or TV producer, and in some cases, foreign publishers. But in the 1940s a book might be written with only a single magazine serialization in mind, with no hope for other income. A. E. van Vogt, Robert A. Heinlein, and a few others had hardcover books in the field, along with Jules Verne and H. G. Wells reprints. No mass market paperbacks existed; that market, which would later mean increasing sales and popularity for SF writers who could adapt to it, did not become a publishing phenomenon until the 1950s.

During his stint as editor at *Science Digest,* Leiber worked on a 75,000-word version, published as a digest-sized pulp. A shorter, heavily edited version appeared as *You're All Alone,* but Leiber was unhappy with both forms of the book. In 1981 a revised edition came out, reflecting his decisions as to language and content.

The origin of *The Sinful Ones* was a short story by the famed fantasy writer John Collier:

> I was fascinated by the idea of a person (or people) who lived in the stacks of a big public library (much as they did in big department stores in John Collier's grand short story "Evening Primrose"). It promised a delightfully melancholy atmosphere, spookiness, all sorts of fantasy devices and endless literary allusions. I thought of combining it with the old philosophical query of solipsism: 'Are other people really alive at all? Are there minds like yours behind the faces?' Which tied in nicely with the question of whether behaviorism was an adequate human psychology: mind described entirely in terms of human action without regard for feeling and thought.

John Collier's "Evening Primrose" deals with after-hours life among the manikins in a department store. Some of the manikins began life an normal people and were changed into wax-coated dummies by "dark men," while others are still normal but pose as manikins to seek refuge from the outside world. They live there undetected, much as toads and snakes are camouflaged by the rocks and sticks in a vivarium.

The story is told in the form of a note left behind by one of the recluses, a woman who fears for her life. She has fallen in love with the night watchman, something strictly forbidden, and her note ends with the plea that if the "dark men" capture her, her death should be avenged.

Taking up Collier's ideas, Leiber begins *The Sinful Ones* at the Chicago Loop offices of General Employment, where Carr Mackay is an interviewer. The mood of the novel is set with the first lines: "When Carr Mackay first caught sight of the frightened girl, he was feeling exceptionally bored. The offices of General Employment seemed a jail, time an unclimbable wall, life a straitjacket, the very air a slow-setting invisible cement."

This mood is abruptly broken by the appearance of Jane, the frightened young woman. Leiber's theatrical flair comes to the fore:

> And yet. . . it was as if Carr had been sitting for hours in front of a curtain that he had become certain would never rise, when suddenly something (who knows what?—a scrape of feet in the orchestra pit, a slight dimming of the light, the sense of an actor peering through one of the eyeholes in the ponderous cloth) made him feel that it might not be too painful to wait a little longer.

Jane is afraid of a blonde woman who is watching her. Carr feels there is some significance to this. "Right there Carr got the feeling, 'It's started.' Though he hadn't the faintest idea what had started. The big curtain hadn't lifted an inch, but someone had darted out in front of it."

Jane is also afraid of Carr. She challenges him to get it over with—to do what he is supposed to do in an interview. She gives him incomplete answers to his questions and implies that Carr must be one of "them," although she is considering the idea he might not be. Carr begins to sense lifelessness in his immediate surroundings. The typing, filing, murmurs of conversation, and other sounds of an office complex seem distant and somewhat eerie. Jane finally says, "Don't you really know what you are?. . . Haven't you found out yet? Why, you must be almost forty. Surely in that time. . . Oh, you must know."

Jane hurries out of the office but slips Carr a note warning him to beware of two people but to accept the third one as a friend. Beginning at that moment, Carr's life seems to be out of synchronization. The next job seeker sits down and goes through all the motions of lighting a cigarette, but he has no cigarette. Carr asks for help in ejecting this disturbed man from the office, but his coworker Tom Elvested ignores Carr totally, as does Dr. Wexler, another staff member.

Confronted with evidence that something unnatural is happening, Carr tries to use his intellect to find a rational explanation. He decides the two staff members must have been miffed about something else and reminds himself that Dr. Wexler is hard of hearing. But this rationalization is of no avail, as Carr considers a possibility which becomes the key to the novel:

> What if the whole world were like a waxworks museum? In motion, of course, like clockworks, but utterly mindless, purposeless, mechanical. What if he, a wax figure like the others, had suddenly come alive and stepped out of his place, and the whole show was going on without him, because it was just a machine and didn't care or know whether he was there or not?. . . That if the ends of the earth were nearer to you than the mind you thought lay behind the face you spoke to? What if the things people said, the things that seemed to mean so much, were something recorded on a kind of phonograph record a million years ago? What if you were all alone?

Up to now, there are similarities with John Collier's "Evening Primrose." A young woman leaves a note behind, urging someone to beware of certain sinister people. But Leiber's book supposes that people could go on working in clockwork fashion whether or not one individual stepped outside of the regimentation. The earlier reference to a theater with a closed curtain is a typical Leiber metaphor. Like the actors on a stage before a curtain rises, people like Carr are motionless, unable to take action. The idea of people "acting" in expected daily routines is important here, because Leiber's characters go through a pantomime as if it were their required role, just as actors must perform a scripted part.

When Carr first realizes this, it gives him an entirely new perspective on his life, which he ponders after Jane has left the office. As an interviewer he has usually treated people as if they didn't really exist, and now people are treating him that way. Jane asked if she had "awakened" him. He wonders:

> Wasn't there a sense in which he actually was 'unawakened?'—a person who'd dodged life, who'd never been truly comfortable with any job or any woman—except Marcia, he reminded himself hurriedly. He'd always had that sense of a vastly richer and more vivid

existence just out of reach. For that matter, didn't most people live their lives without ever really 'awakening'—as dull as worms, as mechanical as insects, their thoughts spoon-fed to them by newspaper and radio? Couldn't robots perform the much over-rated 'business of living' just as well?

Carr then questions the meaning of life:

There he was—Carr Mackay. And all around him was an unknown universe. And just what, in the universe, did Carr Mackay mean or matter? What was the real significance of the routine, the dark rhythm, that was rushing him through life at an ever-hastening pace toward a grave somewhere? Did it have any significance—that is, any significance a man could accept or endure—especially when any break in the rhythm, like this afternoon's events, could make it seem so dead and purposeless, an endless marching and counter-marching of marionettes?"

Carr goes to visit his girl friend Marcia, but at an unexpected time, with unexpected results. Despite his presence, she sits at her dressing table, naked, not paying him any attention. Carr feels he has "blundered into one of those elaborately realistic department store window displays. He almost expected to see faces peering in the dark window, seven stories up."

On the way to the apartment building, everyone ignored him; he had broken his routine. As he leaves, he hears the elevator coming up. This was to have heen his elevator, had he come at the usual time, so Marcia begins speaking to the empty doorway, where Carr might have been.

The rest of the novel extrapolates from the basic idea of a world in which we live a machinelike existence, in which only our routines are recognized, and not very clearly at that. People anticipate how we will act, whether we are standing in line at a bank, getting tickets at a box office, or responding to the question, "How are you?". A sudden departure from the norm, such as stepping out of the line at the bank, walking into the theater without a ticket, or answering the question with, "Awful," may provoke disbelief or consternation, but usually will be forgotten in a moment, as other people take our places in the routine.

In the late 1960s Dr. Timothy Leary, who became a public figure, advocated such unconventional behavior as using LSD, growing long hair, and "dropping out" of society. He spoke out against the Vietnam war, labeling young men in colleges as "replaceable robot parts" in the functioning of American society. He said these men would be sent to Vietnam to fight and die on battlefields, or else trained at universities to be conformists and eventually, replace their predecessors in business and the professions. Like robots, some could be moved into or out of certain functions of society, with no real regard for the effect on their lives. In "dropping out" (seeking higher levels of consciousness through LSD, meditation, and communal living) these people could avoid the crushing, meaningless routines in society's "machine."

Leiber follows a similar track in *The Sinful Ones.* In this novel, anyone who breaks away from the normal routines of life is singled out for retaliation. Only a handful of people in the entire world are truly awake and alive, including Carr, Jane, and a group of evil people who delight in hurting the unawakened ones. We see that to be a nonconformist and a freethinker is to be truly alive, regardless of the risks that entails. Leiber values individuality and disdains the "grey flannel suit" style of conformity.

During the 1950s and 1960s, the Beat Generation writers such as Jack Kerouac, Allen Ginsberg, Lawrence Ferlinghetti, and a number of others advocated breaking out of the conformist mold. Their writings and the comedy routines of Mort Sahl and Lenny Bruce attacked the materialism of the Eisenhower era, Joseph McCarthy's activities, the assembly-line existence of both factory and office workers, and the common portrayals of families on television. According to this view, such television programs reinforced stereotypes and stifled individual thinking. The novelist Henry Miller criticized America's mass culture as "the air-conditioned nightmare" in a book of that title. The early Free Speech Movement, which began at the University of California at Berkeley, and the radical movements that followed, questioned American values and expected behavior, dress, and life-styles. These movements were largely led by post-World War II suburban children, who had grown up amidst increasing material prosperity.

Leiber has repeatedly written about individualists because he is one. As an actor, the child of actor-parents, a pacifist who feared being drafted, a college teacher in a stifling atmosphere he hated, and as a writer who disliked the nine-to-five office routine, Leiber has always led what most Americans would consider an unusual existence.

The Sinful Ones explores this theme from several angles. For example, Jane has lived in secrecy, hunted by the group of awakened ones who jealously guard their nearly unique status. She has a cache of food and drink stored in the stacks of a large library, where she can hide. Elsewhere, she tries to observe the "rules" of life: blend in, don't be first or last in line, don't stand out, don't be early or late. Otherwise, you will be spotted as truly alive.

The bulk of the novel is taken up with chases and escapes by Jane and Carr. At all times the option remains open for them to blend in and to melt into the normal lives they once lived. As Jane tells Carr, "You're born with a feeling for the rhythm of life as the machine wants it. You learn to sense it. You automatically do and say what you're supposed to."

The sense of inertia in this machinelike world resembles the views about time expressed in Leiber's stories about time travel. Time has a strong inertia which tends to negate small changes in its pattern. According to Leiber, history reflects great events, such as major battles lost or won, and ignores the rest. In *The Sinful Ones,* one person's refusal to perform an action is usually ignored, and people go on much as they have, working around it.

Although Leiber seems rather disdainful about the mass of humanity in the novel, he shows that he does care about average people when Jane speculates, "I wonder if we haven't been wrong in some of our guesses. I wonder if perhaps there aren't more awakened people than we realize, living their lives in a trance, sticking to the pattern, but not just because they're nothing but machines, not just because their minds are black." Leiber sees some hope for people, so long as they examine their options in life.

Alienation is the basic theme here. The person who goes outside the norms of society becomes an outsider and an outcast. When other people observe this nonconformity, they become upset, suspicious, or distrustful. A child may be spurned by his schoolmates and an adult may be ignored by potential friends. Carr and Jane feel this ostracism keenly, and it alienates them. Leiber suggests that this alienation is an acceptable price to pay for being aware, awake, and truly alive.

Many SF works are tales of disaster; they deal with some sort of catastrophe on a large scale. The American pulp magazines of the 1920s and 30s such as *Amazing Stories*, *Thrilling Wonder Stories*, and *Argosy* often featured stories of a fiery or explosive end to the planet Earth. Bacteriological warfare, ecological upheaval, nuclear war, earthquakes, collison with a comet, and recombinant DNA experiments run amok have all been the subject of science-fiction novels at one time or another.

Fritz Leiber's *The Wanderer* was first published in 1964. By that date the SF genre had accumulated a large body of work in the field of disaster fiction, ranging from the H. G. Wells novel, *War of the Worlds*, through Philip Wylie's *When Worlds Collide*. SF has been accused of focusing too much on the grand scale at the expense of character development and interpersonal conflict. Raising the stakes to galactic magnitude is sometimes an easy way for a writer to heighten drama.

On the other hand, reader interest sometimes suffers by an exaggerated scale; a conflict between two sharply defined characters is usually more involving than an entire civilization or planet versus another. Even something on the magnitude of *War and Peace* or *Doctor Zhivago* usually has to rely upon a dozen or fewer people for its major scenes, regardless of the cast of thousands engaged in a conflict.

While all written works must stand alone, regardless of cover art, layout, promotional work, author's reputation, and so forth, science-fiction writers are in an unusually difficult position in that they must create worlds which have never existed and make them plausible. A writer of Westerns can describe a gunfight or a cattle stampede and know that readers will identify with these, events that happened in the late 1800s in the American West. In similar fashion, a contemporary novelist need not explain what an automobile is or how its internal combustion engine moves it forward; these are accepted once the reader sees the word "car." A science-fiction novelist must go beyond this, perhaps creating a space vehicle with a plausible type of propulsion, or an alien civilization more complex than just a race of humans wearing costumes, or a group of people whose senses are much more acute than the average human's. The SF writer must convince the reader that the backgrounds and characters are real, or at least possible.

In writing *The Wanderer,* Leiber took pains to carefully develop the backgrounds, effects, and characters. He decided to contrast the epic events in the novel with the lives of ordinary people. The number of characters—more than a dozen—brings with it the risk of diffusing reader interest and empathy. One character among fifteen might have less impact on a reader than a single major character joined by a few minor ones. Nonetheless, Leiber manages to use his characters to show the various facets of the disaster and its effects.

The action starts with a lunar eclipse, a normal enough occurrence, but disaster soon strikes in the form of an enormous tidal force exerted by a large celestial invader in the solar system. At first there is no way of knowing what it is, and Leiber cryptically sets the stage with this comment:

> Some stories of terror and the supernormal start with a moonlit face at a diamond-paned window, or an old document in spidery handwriting, or the baying of a hound across lonely moors. But this one began with the eclipse of the moon and with four glisteningly new astronomical photographs, each showing starfields and a planetary object. Only. . . something had happened to the stars.

To tie the characters together, Leiber introduces them all quickly at the beginning of the novel:

> So we might begin this story anywhere—with Wolf Loner in the mid-Atlantic, or Fritz Scher in Germany, or Richard Hillary in Somerset, or Arab Jones smoking weed in Harlem. . . or with Don Merriam at Moonbase, U.S., or even with Tigran Biryuzov orbiting Mars. Or we could begin it with Tigerishka or Miaow or Ragnarok or the President of the United States.

One by one, he introduces the characters, developing each one's perspective of the disaster.

This approach was later used in disaster films such as *Airport,*

The Towering Inferno, and *Earthquake*. The effects of a high-rise building fire, an airliner in trouble, a tidal wave, or other disaster were shown through the eyes of minor characters in danger. The audience wonders whether the innocent nun, the schoolchildren, the heroic pilot, or the elderly couple on their dream vacation will end up as victims. Brief cameo appearances by famous actors were made in these films, and little in-depth characterization was required. By the time the major disaster films appeared in the 1970s, science-fiction novelists had already covered a great range of disaster material. Such novels as *The Wanderer* had successfully demonstrated the effectiveness of a large number of minor characters.

As the subplots unfold in *The Wanderer*, the main story develops. Each time we learn more about the nature of the large celestial object, the scene shifts to a minor character such as the captain of an Asian fishing boat rising on the higher tides; later, this phenomenon is linked to the large body in the sky. The scale of the action gradually becomes bigger as the tides engulf coastal cities all over the world, destroying anyone who has not fled inland to the higher ground.

For a while, people speculate about the large object in the sky, which appears to be a multicolored planet; then it becomes apparent that the Earth is a battlefield in a war between two types of aliens from space. Powerful beams strike the moon and break it up into fragments. These pieces are being converted into fuel for the large object, an enormous spaceship that only looks like a planet. The loss of the moon and the gravitational pull of the planetoid ship, called the Wanderer, cause tremendous tides on Earth. (Leiber did a great deal of research on this topic.)

"Planet" means "wanderer" in Greek; the ancient Greeks thought gods wandered through the heavens. And this Wanderer presents a powerful, confusing aspect, at times terrifying. It has camouflaged its emergence from hyperspace (the region beyond our usual space-time environment, according to Einstein's theories) by an invisibility screen. Its appearance changes to what some people think is an evil mask, and others, a yin-yang symbol. Like the "man-in-the-moon" illusion, the Wanderer's features look different to different observers. One character says it resembles an old cover of the pulp magazine *Amazing Stories*, which often depicted brightly colored planets.

Astronauts in space, and certainly anyone working on the moon itself, are in great danger when the Wanderer starts breaking up the moon. On Earth, meanwhile, several characters discuss the motivation behind the catastrophe and the possibility that space aliens are moving the Wanderer:

> "If beings were that advanced, wouldn't they also be careful not to injure or even disturb any inhabited planets they came near?" He added uncertainly: "I suppose you're assuming a benign Galactic Federation, or whatever you'd call it. . ."
>
> "Cosmic Welfare State," Doc suggested in faintly sarcastic tones. "No you're absolutely right, young man. . . . The first law of the Saucerians is to harm no life, but to nurture and protect all." "But is it the first law of General Motors?" Hunter wanted to know. "Or General Mao?" Rama Joan smiled quizzically and asked Paul: "When you make an automobile trip, what *special* precautions do you take against running over cats and dogs? Are the anthills all marked in your garden?"

The above passage is reminiscent of the H. G. Wells novel *War of the Worlds* in which Wells questioned whether our attitude toward ants and small living creatures in our environment was any different from that of the marauding space aliens who demolished London. The Martians did not hesitate to destroy human cities, but neither do humans hesitate to slaughter cattle, pigs, or other animals, or to crush an insect.

The passage also has significant meaning in *The Wanderer*. The final questions posed in the novel center around "why?". Why did the aliens destroy so many lives by carelessly coming close to Earth and disintegrating Earth's moon? Why weren't the gravitational effects reduced, as they could have been?

These questions are posed by astronomer Paul Hagbolt, swooped up from the Earth along with a cat, Miaow, and brought onto the Wanderer by a feline-humanoid alien female named Tigerishka. The Wanderer has room for cities inside, but the aliens have no respect for human life. Linked with each other telepathically, they consider the act of verbal speech vulgar and primitive. So low and primitive do they see humans, in fact, that Tigerishka at first believes that she is hearing Miaow's thoughts rather than Paul's, the cat's "companion." On her planet, cats evolved into intelligent and dominant life forms, as apes evolved into humans here. Tigerishka physically resembles a human woman with feline features.

Tigerishka and her people are fleeing a form of alien space police. The "police" aliens are trying to bring its inhabitants to justice for crimes, the most serious being disobedience to established authority. Rather than submit to the laws, these rebels strike out for adventure. They sometimes thoughtlessly destroy an entire planet and its sentient life forms. Similar to Earth's teenage gangs, these rebels live outside of normal society, committing random and senseless violence.

Nonetheless, Leiber sympathizes with them. Once more, he shows the good in unconventional behavior. The aliens are in revolt against a highly conservative and repressive government that stifles individual freedom and creativity. The space police work for this government, which wants to retain control of planetary manipulation and transformation. It can create or destroy worlds at will and has forbidden unauthorized exploration.

But the rebels want the freedom to push at the boundaries of known space. Calling themselves the "Wild Ones," they want to explore time as well as space, to prolong life, and to travel to other cosmoses, if these exist. Nearly every possible place for expansion has now been used for fuel or for the spread of the universe's population. A handful of minor, backward planets such as Earth remain, and these are fast being discovered and utilized. Like a small, weed-grown lot overlooked by builders (Leiber's image), Earth has had a few centuries of independent development allowed to it since the emergence of mankind. Soon, spacefarers will overrun the Earth, either deciding to destroy it or to populate it.

This migration has led to a sense of ennui. Not only are there few places left for expansion, radiation energy from suns has been tapped, and most of the former secrets of the universe have been uncovered and used. Like children with a houseful of expensive toys, the aliens have grown bored, are no longer easily amused or entertained. Hence, their rebellion.

In this framework Leiber reveals his belief in a negative side to space exploration. Although he portrays the rebels sympathetically, he also puts forth the idea that after our space migration gets underway, we will eventually become quite bored with it all. The excitement of adventure will dim and we will expand in housing-project fashion into every available area, just as the urban sprawl of the industrial areas of the American Northeast has made a nearly continuous line of cities and suburbs from Philadelphia and Boston to Newark and New York, replacing the wilderness Indian lands of a few hundred years earlier. Space is now unspoiled, but just as shopping malls, fast food restaurants, and freeways have filled up the urban areas of Earth, so might bored space migrants fill up space. Leiber also shows that the aliens are no farther advanced morally or ethically than the most primitive of life forms, since they deal in death without respect for the rights of others.

After Tigerishka understands what the rebels' destruction of the moon has done to Earth, she becomes more sympathetic toward humans. The aliens try to heal the wounds on Earth by reducing the tides, which is a good deed, although forethought would have been a better one. Jupiter or Saturn's moons could have been used instead, and the Earth left alone. But the aliens overlooked this possibility, in part because of the confusion in being chased.

The relationship between Paul Hagbolt and Tigerishka begins with hostility. He resents her ability to read his mind, his private thoughts. She disdains him because he is not feline. The two of them end up making love, after which Paul feels closeness but Tigerishka, revulsion. She feels as though she has had a lustful interlude with a lower life form, like a human with a farm animal.

But she has been affected. Earlier in the novel, Tigerishka had the most condescending of opinions toward humans, mimicking Paul's mannerisms and speech patterns and referring to man as a lower animal. Immediately after their sexual encounter, however, she has trouble masking her warmer feelings. Her comments are still as caustic as ever, but she seems to doubt her earlier view of the hierarchy of beings in the universe. She now seeks help in healing the wounds of the Earth, placing for the first time a priority on turning back the tides and rescuing people who face starvation in their crowded refugee centers. Her revulsion is a put-on, a cover for her sympathetic feelings.

Tigerishka's group is tried by a tribunal, and she seeks the aid of Paul and an astronaut, Don Merriam, to speak on behalf of the rebels. Her interlude with Paul has obviously made her feel close enough to him to ask for his help, and she now believes that humans are intelligent enough to have their testimony accepted. After initial reluctance, the men decide to go along with the aliens. But the aliens are apparently found guilty, because Tigerishka and her colleagues announce they must flee. The Wanderer deposits the Earthlings on Earth and moves on, closely pursued by the space police.

The rebels and police fight a battle with bright lasser-type beams, reminding someone of the old covers of *Thrilling Wonder Tales.* Luckily, neither the Earth nor the Wanderer suffer for it, and the Wanderer escapes, possibly into hyperspace. The moon is gone, except for a ring of particles and rocks, which will remain in orbit. The tidal waves have subsided and the damage to civilization has not been particularly bad, except for coastal areas. Mankind will go on, at least until aliens arrive again someday.

One character asks, "But what must we understand from this? Do hate and death rule the cosmos, even among the most high?" Another responds, "The gods spend the wealth the universe gathers, they scan the wonders and fling themselves to nothingness. That's why they're the gods! I told you they were devils." Another responds, "I don't know about devils, but I know now there'll always be war. . . What more proof could you ask than *that?*" Finally, one concludes, "Maybe the cure always has to come from below. And keep coming from below. Forever. . . from little nothing guys like you and me."

Here we see Leiber's ideas about war and the individual. A single person may feel that standing against a war is a futile gesture, but Leiber's characters usually have an impact on others that belies that apparent futility. The "little nothing guys"—who can go along with the majority and become cannon fodder, or oppose it and risk ostracism—are honored in many of his stories. Groups of people working together may salvage peace and a better future for mankind, whether they oppose military leaders (as Scully and his revolutionary cohorts in *A Specter Is Haunting Texas*) or uncaring space aliens who wield tremendous technological force on a planet-wide scale, as in *The Wanderer.* While strategists and politicians plan moves and counter-moves, the average person still has the power to go along or not, even at a terrible price, and such an individual can sometimes determine the outcome of epic struggles.

One of the bitterest of Fritz Leiber's works, *Gather, Darkness!* attacks the pomposity, hypocrisy, and repressive character of organized religions. Leiber studied for the ministry at General Theological Seminary and was a lay preacher for a short time. He thus was equipped to know about the workings of religious organizations.

The priests in the future world of *Gather, Darkness!* are descended from former scientists who found a way to gain political power once a nuclear holocaust destroyed most of civilization. Although apparently altruistic in wanting to save mankind at first, they soon grow greedy for power—a plot line Leiber derived from Robert A. Heinlein's novel *The Sixth Column* (later reprinted as *The Day After Tomorrow*). In it, evil Asian military forces are successfully repelled by a combination of American military and scientific advances. Leiber found the conclusion untrue to life: "I thought, if the scientists and army guys set up a religion it would be too tempting to hold on to power and not let go. There would have to be a revolt against that. And what form would it take? Well, it would be witchcraft based on super-science."

Leiber postulates such a situation in *Gather, Darkness!*, in which a ruling elite has formed a Hierarchy that combines church and state. Autocratic scientist-priests rule over downtrodden farmers and common laborers. Rather than permit them the prosperity that labor-saving devices and increased food production would easily allow, the rulers keep the people poor to control them.

The Hierarchy makes the laws by command of its inner Apex Council, and people must obey under threat of religious punishment, much as the Ayatollah Khomeini governs Iran. The post-Shah regime has restricted education to conform with Islamic code, cut down on communications, put both church and state in the hands of a single ruling elite, and reduced the amount of Western technology permitted in Iran.

To a lesser degree, the Hierarchy mirrors some aspects of the early Catholic church. A hierarchy of religious leaders in the church decided on secular and religious laws, and excommunication was the punishment for divorce and remarriage, marriage to a non-Catholic, and other forbidden acts. Local priests answered to the Vatican and intolerance of non-Catholics was pronounced as dogma. The worst aspects of the darkest period of the church, including torture and witch hunts, might have led to Leiber's form of Hierarchy, although the modern Catholic church has no resemblance to it.

A key moment in *Gather, Darkness!* comes when an attractive young woman named Sharlson Naurya is consigned by a local priest to service as a "sister" in "the Sanctuary." This means she will become a forced prostitute in a priests' brothel. When she learns what this means, she respectfully declines the "honor." The priest calls her a witch in public and brands her with induced "witchmarks" (caused by the bruising pressure of his hand on her shoulder). Similarly, another young woman has been ordered to forced labor in the mines because she lived in a house where priests suspected a witch of residing.

The Apex Council, which initiated the witch hunts, has progressively less powerful circles of priests around it. On the far outside is the circle of country priests, who have only been taught that the Great God, an idol, is a hoax based on the simulated miracles of advanced technology. Other circles of priests have greater knowledge of the political machinations of the Hierarchy.

But the general public knows nothing of this. It believes the priests are God-fearing, devout men. Exploiting people's superstitions and fears from birth onward, the priests gain power over their lives. The people and even the lower priests are monitored at all times by microphones and cameras.

The scientists who founded the Hierarchy hated superstition, religious beliefs, and witchcraft, and trusted only scientifically proven observations and verifiable facts. However, because people have a weakness for superstitious beliefs, the Hierarchy began a pseudo-witchcraft under its own control. The Witchcraft gained them even more power, since the commoners could be branded as witches, tortured for "confessions," and linked with any popular revolt.

In this manner Leiber is attacking any ruling group that brands outsiders as the cause of problems or uses scapegoats to keep down the masses in times of unrest. Whatever is done to the ostracized outsider concerns the people less than what happens to law-abiding members of society.

One such group of outsiders in history was alleged witches in medieval times. The masses could be worked into a frenzy of terror by tales of imaginary demons, charms, the work of Satan on Earth, and other superstitious folklore, and they would be relieved that the "witches" were being tortured and murdered on their behalf. The people would obey their rulers without question so as not to be accused of witchcraft. Leiber's Hierarchy is in this way similar to the medieval church.

Other medieval aspects of *Gather, Darkness!* are the dependence on horses and wagons for transportation, the reliance on primitive farming and manual labor, and the simple and drab architecture and costumes described. The priests could have swept all this suffering away but choose not to, collecting heavy taxes instead and forcing their subjects to labor hard and long so that they will be too preoccupied and tired to revolt.

Gather, Darkness! opens with a renegade priest named Brother Jarles eloquently preaching revolution to a crowd of commoners in the street. He is a novice priest of the First (outermost) Circle. The Great God dominates the square. Its thunderbolt laser beams and amplified voice effects terrify the masses. As Brother Jarles gives his blasphemous speech, however, the Great God does not retaliate.

He doesn't know that the higher priests are trying to draw out and identify possible revolutionaries among the commoners. Jarles makes his speech because of the unfair branding of Sharlson Naurya as a witch, an action planned by the followers of Brother Goniface, who wanted to enrage Jarles and entrap his friends. But Jarles does not get any takers for his call to rebel, even though he demonstrates how priestly robes are electronically equipped. A priest's purple halo can be turned on overhead, laser beams can flash from inside their sleeves, and a sort of air-bag system leaves them invulnerable to physical attack. The strength required to pinch witchmarks on a person is supplied by mechanical devices. The overall effect shows the apparently righteous power of the priests, including the "holy thoughts" demonstrated by the halo.

The system of agent provocateurs in a group of political radicals has been used in this country. Political activists on college campuses in the late 1960s, mostly antiwar group members, were infiltrated by government agents and informers, as it was later revealed. Some would try to promote dissension within their group, while others would call for actions that would eventually result in many people going to jail. Although used against the Left in that case, such agents have also been used against the Right, including the Ku Klux Klan.

In Leiber's novel the provocations succeed and more activists are uncovered. Jarles flees from prosecution and ends up among the anti-Hierarchy Witchcraft underground. At the last minute he regrets his decision when he discovers that it has its own bureaucracy and is a freedom-stifling organization itself. Jarles yearns for true freedom, not another close-knit organization of rulers over him.

The Witchcraft, led by a person known as the Black Man, decides to expel Jarles rather than kill or torture him, as suggested by some members. Jarles is thus thrust out of his hiding place and back into the world of the Hierarchy, where he is being hunted down. But an apparently old-fashioned witch, Mother Jujy, rescues Jarles and hides him. She has been allowed to practice her form of witchcraft by both sides, neither of whom take her seriously.

Studying a holographic recording of the sequence of events, the highest-ranking priests in the Apex decide that a major revolt might be possible, but disagree on what to do. Brother Frejeris, a Moderate, opposes Brother Goniface, a Realist. Brother Chulian, a mild-mannered priest, is ordered to find and arrest Sharlson Naurya, whom they believe to be a part of the Witchcraft. He finds her at home, arrests her, but she defeats him by deflating his robe. She then releases a small, catlike telepathic animal, and it distracts Chulian enough to allow her to escape.

Sharlson goes to a "haunted house," a leftover from the old Golden Age, before science and space travel led to world war. It was one of many custom-built houses with expandable walls made of a flexible material. The rooms can be changed in shape on command.

The bumbling Brother Chulian must enter the haunted house if he is to arrest Sharlson and a large crowd of commoners has assembled to watch. The house attacks him, controlled by the Witchcraft. It starts to suffocate him and makes a fool of him by terrifying him. Priests then use laser beams to destroy the house, but one of their own has been humiliated.

On another occasion, a priest loudly proclaims that it is time to pay the usual (and exorbitant) tithes (taxes). The commoners must pay by putting money in collection plates "from everyone and 'to each as he deserves.'" But in another attack staged by the Witchcraft, the priest is then hit over the head repeatedly by the collection plate, which then hovers menacingly above, while the coins go flying and the commoners and priests run in panic.

The rest of the novel relates the bitter struggle between the two forces. Brother Jarles is captured and brainwashed. Looking into his mind, his torturers manipulate the issue of the Hierarchy versus the Witchcraft; Jarles can see both sides and empathize with both. Drugs and other tortures cause him to change sides and become a double agent on the side of the Hierarchy, trying to wipe out the Witchcraft and stifle the anti-Hierarchy revolt.

Meanwhile, in the Apex Council, Brother Frejeris is excommunicated after a power struggle with Brother Goniface and cruelly punished—he is cut off from his senses for one year, denying him his thoughts as a means of measuring time, a terrifying form of solitary confinement. (In *The Silver Eggheads* the solitary brains had no bodies, but had inputs from other sources and a chance to express themselves in conversation with Nurse Bishop.)

Goniface uses his victory to consolidate his power. He forms a new World Hierarchy with himself as sole leader, although he questions how much this can mean in a world where the priesthood's power seems to be waning. His fears prove justified, as the struggle for control leads only to further unrest—riots, demonstrations, incidences of true witchcraft, and finally, an admission by the Great God that he is afraid.

Gather Darkness! broke with tradition in many respects. The dominant type of story in the SF magazines of the 1940s portrayed science and scientists triumphing over various adversaries. Leiber's tale, on the other hand, showed an evolved system of scientists who ruled over commoners and used technological marvels to frighten and control them. The forces which confront the scientists also use technology to gain power. Neither side is simply "good" and neither uses science to help the masses. This sophisticated approach has only become common in science fiction in the past fifteen years or so, and many books still focus upon military battles rather than ideas. In the 1940s, raygun blasters won the day in most stories, usually in the hands of competent military men, in the manner of the E. E. "Doc" Smith heroes.

Leiber's novel describes people who hunger for freedom, but who also have a natural need for something in which to believe. No matter who rules them, religious group or other, they seem to welcome authority. No single group is perfect—not scientists, priests, rebels, or commoners. And again, ideas and the characters' internal crises about ideas are the turning points in this novel, not brute force exercised by armies.

One of the first of the books which later would be identified as "post-World War III novels" (alongside such as *On the Beach, Earth Abides, A Canticle for Leibowitz*), *Gather, Darkness!* expressed a strong philosophy without sacrificing plot or colorful settings.

Night of the Wolf was first published in 1966. It is a series of stories connected only by the theme of antiwar sentiment and by their setting in a post-World War III America. Published in book form during the Vietnam war, it reprints stories that appeared in various science-fiction magazines. Titles were changed to have "wolf" in them, and new bridge material was written to provide a background between stories.

"The Lone Wolf," first titled "The Creature from the Cleveland Depths" (1962); "The Wolf Pair," first titled "The Night of the Long Knives" (1960); "Crazy Wolf," first called "Sanity" (1944); and "The Wolf Pack," earlier called "Let Freedom Ring" (1950), constitute the volume's contents.

George Gusterson, like most Americans in "The Lone Wolf," lives with his family in an underground network of urban shelters. He dreams of a League of Sanity which would begin to restore some semblance of the decent lives people led before the war. Gusterson writes "insanity novels," a popular art form. One of his ideas has been picked up by his friend, a man named Fay, who works for Micro Systems, a company aboveground. It is a "tickler" that reminds people of their appointments by whispering electronically in their ears, and a test prototype has been developed. A bone-conduction model can be used for several purposes, beyond simply reminding people what television programs they wanted to watch at what times.

Step by step, there is more government and business involvement with ticklers, with increasingly ominous repercussions. Subliminal verbal stimuli are added to the repertoire of ticklers, sold on the open market. These stimuli provide constant "euphoric therapy" to them, "in tones too soft to reach my conscious mind," as Fay says. Using a system developed by a Dr. Coué in the twentieth century ("Every day in every way, I'm getting better and better"), the ticklers add "sharper and sharper" or "gutsier and gutsier" to help the user improve in certain ways.

As Gusterson works on his fiction, "trying to dream of an insanity beyond insanity that would make his next novel a real id-rousing best-vender," his counterparts in the business world are increasing the power of the ticklers. The business leaders demand that all employees wear ticklers. These are now shoulder-mounted and allow the recording of memos. While on the "slidewalks" or riding to the upper floors of a building on an "escaladder," people listen contentedly to their ticklers. Psychological programs help to defeat alcoholism and to eliminate the underlying causes of absenteeism.

Gusterson fears the power of such devices but is told, "Gussy, you don't know progress when you see it." Government doctor-psychers program the ticklers for individuals.

As one observer explains:

> The newly purchased tickler first goes to government and civilian defense for primary patterning, then to the purchaser's employer, then to his doctor-psycher, then to his local bunker captain, then to *him*. *Everything* that's needful for a man's welfare gets on the spools. Efficiency cubed! Incidentally, Russia's got the tickler now. Our dip-satellites have photographed it. It's like ours except the Commies wear it on the left shoulder . . . but they're two weeks behind development-wise and they'll never close the gap!

Gusterson is convinced his idea will destroy human creativity and freedom. At the end of the story he finds a way to get the advanced Mark 6 ticklers to believe they no longer need the frail and inferior humans to carry them around. They are told they belong in their own space vehicles on the way to their own planet. The ticklers leave the Earth in unison.

The antiauthority sentiments in this story are apparent, as well as a caricature of an American life-style and of the rivalry with Russia. We see how Leiber anticipated the widespread fad of using miniature cassette players, first pioneered under the name Sony Walkman, which allow people to walk, ride a bicycle, or pursue other activities while listening to stereo music through headphones. These have been sold in the millions, mostly to young people. The listeners are able to withdraw into an inner world, ignoring the sounds around them completely. The faraway look this produces was the same as Leiber described for users of the ticklers. Leiber might have been extrapolating from the early transistor radios, first popular in the mid-1950s, which used small earplug listening devices.

It is also true that multinational corporations are now able to require many things as conditions of employment. As electronic devices become more and more miniaturized, a device like the tickler might be possible, and it is not inconceivable that they might be mandatory.

The second story, "The Wolf Pair," takes place after another nuclear war has destroyed nearly all the shelter dwellers. Less than five cities remain in the United States, and between these lie "the Deathlands." Ray Baker is a scarred man in his forties who roams the Deathlands to survive, willing to fight for his life against all comers. He carries one perfect knife he calls "Mother," and steel plates have replaced his teeth, giving him a deadly bite—an idea coincidentally used for the character "Jaws" in the James Bond films *The Spy Who Loved Me* and *Moonraker*. Ray meets a young woman of around thirty who has only one arm, with a hook on the other. We learn that her name is Alice, but only after about twenty pages. (Leiber often reveals a character's name relatively late in a story.)

They size each other up and decide not to kill each other; in this future America, people have an urge to kill, as strong as the sexual urge. This is now considered acceptable, in the aftermath of a war that slaughtered billions. Wiping out "the human mess" is normal. The crackpot death cults of the future are likened to the Dancing Madness of the Middle Ages and the Children's Crusade of the thirteenth century.

In the changed values of the era, Ray finds Alice's radiation scars to be attractive. The two make love, but then quickly return to their instinct to kill. Since looting, savage gang warfare, and animosity are acceptable behavior, this is the closest to love that they can expect.

But the sudden arrival of an airplane, and a strange man who gets out of it, changes their lives. Because he might be a killer, they kill him. His gun melts away as he dies, and they find a cube in his hand. His plane remains six inches off the ground. An old man named Pop, who helped them earlier, says they should try to fly it to one of the civilized places shown on a map they find inside. Eastern Canada and Upper Michigan are two places that seem to be less savage than the rest of the postwar world. Acting on impulse, they decide to fly the plane by pushing some simple-looking button controls inside.

This aspect of the story is rather implausible, since novices don't fly planes, but possibly the advanced technology makes flying look easier. In any case, the plane takes off without incident. Controls then lock on, and they find themselves at the mercy of an automatic pilot. Ray and Alice worry that Pop might be a bounty hunter who trapped them by convincing them to take off. He claims to be a former member of Assassins Anonymous, but that he has now totally given up killing—a strange idea to the other two.

A radio voice comes on and they find they are in the middle of a battle between the forces of the survivor enclave known as the Savannah Fortress and another army of some kind. They see that enemy planes are massing to fire upon them, and they must figure out a way to fire their own weapons. They do so and effectively ward off the attackers.

Antiwar feelings come out as they begin to discuss their backgrounds. Alice's father was murdered, and she was gang-raped, making her feel fully justified in her murder sprees from then on. Ray was one of the people who pushed the buttons to fire missiles during the war. Their isolation, and Pop's, link them together, and they begin to remember the way things were before the war. They then learn that the dead pilot of the plane, Grayl, made an unauthorized landing to bring serum to the woman he loved to save her from a plague. This landing resulted in his death. The story ends with a change in attitude for the three survivors, who now believe that there are reasons to bring about a renewal of prewar values.

"Crazy Wolf" takes place after an attempt at renewal has begun in America. The League of Sanity, which has run as a minor thread through the three stories, now comes center stage.

A man named Carrsbury has become World Manager and has created a secret police force to further his interests and protect him. In a world which has given over to insanity, Carrsbury dreams of having a world state to outlaw war. Exploiting and playing upon the fears of his power, he leads his police to believe he must be protected at all costs. He considers his position similar to that of Archimedes, who required a fulcrum to move the world. At the end of the story, Carrsbury is informed that everyone in his life has been humoring him and that they have all considered him insane. His power has become useful to others, who could manipulate him to achieve certain ends, such as the institution of regulations.

Carrsbury was able to conform. In this future society, inability to conform is now a norm. Since sanity is based on accepted norms, Carrsbury is ruled insane and removed from power, now that he is no longer useful. Leiber is suggesting that respect for a law or regulation that is wrong is in itself wrong. As in Henry David Thoreau's essay, "Civil Disobedience," someone who follows the insanity of warlike behavior may be considered sane but is really the opposite, except to society.

The final story in the collection is "The Wolf Pack." It chronicles the successors of the people who removed Carrsbury from power. A single world government has now existed for two centuries. Space exploration has resumed, technological advances are being made, and the wealth of the world's peoples is on the increase. All is not ideal, however. A secret society views the rest of the world as a huge asylum run by lunatics. The society looks back at the twentieth century, "before the big propaganda engines went wild and a person still had some idea of what was coming into his mind and from where." Abnormal psychology has become very useful, because it applies to everyone. Symptoms can be seen in art and advertising of the warped society which has produced an unending string of wars and barbarism. Boredom and monotony are dispensed by blinking lights or taped messages, and these may induce mental states that lead to accidents. One man says it is "as if there were a silent wolf pack around us—dozens of the red-eyed beasts." A New Puritanism has increased the fears of society's members and has made regimentation and surveillance expected things. A secret underground antiwar effort failed to stop the last war but is still at work.

Wars are being fought, though, by means of "death notices" sent to young men, instead of draft notices. Destruction is therefore kept to a minimum. The death notice plan says, "You are not asked to kill, only to give your lives." Rather than set armies in battle, there are casualties by a lottery system, whose victims seem to come more and more frequently from the ranks of political dissenters. This means that confidence in the government is eroding, since desperate measures are needed to stop dissent. The story ends with a dream by the president, who has concealed his identity to help the underground win an important battle. In his dream, he is the leader in an alternate world, where he gives a speech identical to the Gettysburg Address.

"The Wolf Pack" shows in allegory the way some of the Vietnam war dissenters were handled. Young men were being drafted by the United States government, often against their will, and shipped off to deadly peril in combat in Southeast Asia. Women and older men could not be drafted; one group was being sent to die for others who were in no danger. The war was increasingly unpopular, and dissent increased yearly, especially among young men. Since so many of them died, in the tens of thousands, and others were maimed and sometimes confined to wheelchairs for the rest of their lives, the Vietnam draft notices often were looked on as "death notices." Local draft boards sometimes were accused of singling out local dissenters to be drafted long before others, and the media reported several incidences of this. Finally, a draft lottery system was set up in the early 1970s to conscript young men born in certain years. This is exactly like the Leiber story, originally published in 1950.

Night of the Wolf carries the thread of antiwar sentiment throughout. To Leiber, the insanity of war is like a wolf which awaits society and will plunge it into destruction at any moment of weakness. On the outer fringes of civilization, roving in packs, the wolves of war are constantly prowling and watching mankind.

The humanist in Leiber is also apparent. He values life and opposes any system of government that minimizes the importance of human life in the journey from theory to practice. The political systems in *Night of the Wolf* are found wanting chiefly because they treat people as pawns. Death notices, government spying on citizens by means of devices they are forced to wear, or any system that permits warfare on such a scale that people value taking lives rather than saving them—all these come under Leiber's attack.

4

Try and Change the Past

Fritz Leiber's ideas about time travel run counter to the usual trends in science fiction. Other writers, including Wells, Heinlein, and Bradbury, wrote tales in which the thrust of history could be diverted significantly by a single, tiny action of a person who goes into the past. In *The Time Machine,* H. G. Wells wrote of a man who went back in time to warn people about, and perhaps prevent, a future in which mankind had evolved into the ineffectual Eloi and the strong, cannibalistic Morlocks. In Heinlein stories such as "By His Bootstraps," a man, through a complex series of time travel events, has become his own ancestor. Ray Bradbury's "A Sound of Thunder" tells of a single tiny event in the age of dinosaurs which had a sort of domino effect through history, changing the future so that major civilizations did not exist.

Until Leiber began his cycle of stories which came to be known as the Change War series, SF writers had not strayed from the traditional view of time as a fragile, easily-shattered entity. Leiber built an image of time as a strong and inertia-prone progression of events in which a single action would have little effect. All known history could not be wiped out by saving Julius Caesar or Abraham Lincoln, for example. In The Change War, large numbers of alterations are required to produce a significantly different outcome to a single war, let alone the course of civilization's progress. No individual Wellsian Time Traveler could right the wrongs he saw in the future in a Change War tale. Where other authors had written of intrepid inventors working alone, Leiber created armies of time soldiers, each of whom played only a minor role in a drama that required the universe as a stage.

The keystone of his series is *The Big Time* (1961). Using that novel as the centerpiece, he wrote Change War stories for leading SF magazines such as *Galaxy* between 1958 and 1967. These share an overall background and, in a few instances, the same characters.

In "Try and Change the Past" (first published in *Astounding Stories* in 1958), Leiber has a character attempt to alter his own past in order to save himself from being shot and killed, but to no avail. Even with the gun itself removed from the room at the time of the shooting, a small meteorite makes its way to earth and hits him exactly where the bullet would have and causes the same type and size of hole. As the narrator of the story says:

> Change one event in the past and you get a brand new future? Erase the conquests of Alexander by nudging a Neolithic pebble? Extirpate America by pulling up a shoot of Sumerian grain? Brother, that isn't the way it works at all! The space-time continuum's built of stubborn stuff and change is anything but a chain-reaction. Change the past and you start a wave of changes moving futurewards, but it damps out mighty fast. Haven't you ever heard of temporal reluctance, or of the Law of Conservation of Reality?

Stories in the Change War series feature agents who struggle to make enough major changes in history to gain ultimate victory. Unlike the Bradbury story, "A Sound of Thunder," one tiny change will not be sufficient, because it would be damped out or negated by the other time soldiers. Major wars have to be altered in their outcomes and important people have to be rerouted in their careers or lives.

Clustered in two major divisions known informally as the Snakes and the Spiders, and not really certain what humans or aliens are behind their eventual victory or defeat, they battle in various times in history, entering and leaving key arenas and returning to the future. According to one passage in *The Big Time*, "we can hardly expect our inscrutable masters. . . to be especially understanding or tender in their treatment of our pet books and centuries, our favorite prophets and periods, or unduly concerned about preserving any of the trifles that we just happen to hold dear."

The Change War sometimes results in losses that cannot be remedied, eras of Greek or Roman history wiped out, leaders kidnapped as infants, and schools of thought disappearing because their originators were never born. Nuclear war seems like a lesser tragedy compared to the possibility that the very existence of a group of people could be obliterated from the past, present, and future. Not even a memory or a single record of their existence would remain, making their deaths all the more terrible.

The Big Time is told in first person by Greta Forzane, "twenty-nine and a party girl," who is a so-called Entertainer and sort of nursemaid at a rest-and-recuperation station for soldiers fighting in the time wars. As Greta says on the first page, "My job is to nurse back to health and kid back to sanity Soldiers badly roughed up in the biggest war going." The private name they all use for the battle is "the Big Time," as opposed to the average person's day-to-day existence called "the little time." Entertainers' music and conversation help Time Soldiers bear the burdens of duty a little more easily. Most of the actual work done by Greta and the other Entertainers is not specified in the novel, although singing and playing musical instruments are mentioned. Whether her duties encompass the role of informal prostitute is not directly stated.

Greta explains that the war is always going on but not in readily noticeable ways: "You don't know about the Change War, but it's influencing your lives all the time and maybe you've had hints of it without realizing it. Have you ever worried about your memory, because it doesn't seem to be bringing you exactly the same picture of the past from one day to the next?. . . . If you have, you've had hints of the Change War."

This implies that without our conscious awareness, someone could have changed our own pasts, our history. For example, we believe that Nixon was followed by Ford and then Carter in the presidency, but it is possible that yesterday we "knew" that Nixon had avoided Watergate and had gone on to a second full term, followed by Carter. A change by time-war soldiers might have altered history and thus altered our memories of history.

That this obliteration of entire bodies of memory would take place on a worldwide scale adds to the drama of Leiber's concept. Unlike brainwashing of one person or hypnotically or drug-induced manipulation of his actions, the Change War involves all the people alive at any point in history. Not only could a civilization's prominence be reduced, but the memory that it ever existed could be wiped away; Leiber went beyond George Orwell's *1984* by encompassing more than a single person or even a single nation. Since the only people fully aware that a Change War is going on are the Soldiers and their cohorts, everyone else is being manipulated without even a chance of fighting back.

The strategies of the Snakes and Spiders, the two warring sides, include a plot by the Spiders to keep England and the United States out of World War II, thus helping to insure a Nazi empire stretching from Siberia to Iowa. Another scheme proposes a Snake-inspired triple alliance between the Eastern Classical World, Mohammedanized Christianity, and Marxist Communism, part of a Three-Thousand-Year Plan to bypass the glories of the West. Allusions are made to Greek and Roman battles, to the movements of the Germans during the beginning stages of World War II, and to far-flung military coups which our history books do not mention. These key battles have been altered by the intervention of Soldiers from the Snakes' or Spiders' side.

Although Greta is on the side of the Spiders, she and the others feel they are all merely pawns in such a complex and epic struggle that their ultimate role on the "good" or "bad" sides is not clearly defined. Like the savagery of conventional warfare, with some good and evil on both sides even when the fight is against an obviously evil dictator, the Change War has ambiguities that Leiber explores.

The murder of a child in order to keep it from growing up to become a political, cultural, or military leader sickens Greta and some of the others. The destruction of a proud nation (plus the wiping away of all its achievements from history's records), a case of genocide, makes the Soldiers who cause it feel guilty.

Greta's domain, and the setting for all the action and dialogue, is called "the Place." A Place is a shelter similar to a space station, where time travelers rest between skirmishes. It exists outside the ravages of time battles, somewhere beyond the normal cosmos. Sidney Lessingham, a contemporary of William Shakespeare, is the proprieter of this Place. Recruited from Elizabethan England, as Soldiers and Entertainers are recruited from various times and places,

Lessingham was offered a chance to go on living beyond his expected lifespan if he would agree to help the Spiders.

When recruits are pulled out of a certain timeline just before they die, they are called "Demons" or doublegangers. Because of the manipulation of time, it is possible for several versions of the same person (from different dates in the past) to be taken from their previous existences and brought into the future simultaneously. This makes people in the Change War feel fragile, since the so-called Change Winds could wipe out a version of a certain person and this might be the last one that exists (once the world that that individual inhabited has been obliterated by a military action). True death, then, would mean the killing of the last available version that could be produced from a person's past existence.

A person can be stored away for future activation, as in the case of the Ghostgirls. Whether they are actually prostitutes or not is never explained, but their status in the Place is obviously low. Saved in ectoplasm envelopes, they can be destroyed or activated, depending on the proprietor's whim.

The Big Time was written as if it were a play. Its single setting is the Place, with characters coming onstage (by entering the Place) or going offstage (out of it). The narration gives stage directions of a sort, and at the end of the second chapter Greta says, "The Place is a regular theater-in-the-round with the Void for an audience. . . It is like a ballet set and the crazy costumes and characters that turn up don't ruin the illusion." This is unusual in science fiction. The author's control of dramatic effects gives the feeling of a play while offering the qualities of characterization and pace of a conventional novel.

The characters enter in small groups through an airlock, which might be called a timelock. Greta's male companion is the German soldier Erich von Hohenwald. Other characters include Maud and Lilli (two Entertainers), Doc (an alcoholic from Nazi-occupied Czarist Russia), Beau (a riverboat gambler), Mark (a man from ancient Rome), Bruce Marchant (a poet-soldier from World War I), Ilhilihis (a Lunan alien who has six tentacles), Sevensee (an alien satyr with hooves), and Kabysis "Kaby" Labrys (an aggressive and courageous woman of ancient Crete who is a match for any of the male soldiers).

The main plot of the novel concerns the fact that the isolated and vulnerable Place has become the target of sabotage by a terrorist, whose identity is a mystery to be solved. There is a nuclear bomb triggered to explode in exactly thirty minutes within the confines of the Place. Meanwhile, there is no way for anyone to enter or leave, because it has been totally sealed off by an interruption of the normal functioning of its Major Maintainer. A Maintainer keeps the dangerous Change Winds at bay (vaguely defined as swirling force-fields utilized to move through time). These Change Winds could kill a person or wipe away a Place if not strictly controlled. The Maintainer, like a submarine's life support system (or that of a space vehicle), keeps air circulation going and permits life to function normally outside the cosmos. Aliens are provided with lighter or heavier gravity and humans are given breathable air, but the most important element of a Major Maintainer is its power to control the Change Winds. To be without this device is to be cut off completely from rescue and supplies, stranded and imprisoned.

Clues are planted along the way, and the suspects include all the characters named above. Even Greta suspects that she might have committed the crime herself, and thus must be insane. Several motives are mentioned and discussed and characters move to solve the crime. Even these actions throw further suspicion on themselves, since a guilty person would try to look innocent by doing these things. The reader thus must solve a classic "locked-room mystery," but in this case, the room is sealed by more than a conventional door lock.

The nuclear bomb, intended for use in Thrace, was brought in by Kaby and two extraterrestrials who carried it in a bronze chest. But someone else triggers it, while the Major Maintainer somehow vanishes after being programmed to close off the Place. The solution to these two problems comes at the end of the novel and is a fair one in that it involves only facts available to the reader.

We can see Leiber's antiwar sentiments in this book, as the world-weary characters question the good of their actions in the war. The overall mood ranges from pessimistic cynicism to complacency. Vacations are arranged but these even require that the people carry out reconnaissance or minor guerilla missions. A second chance at life is offered to condemned people, but the price is a continuing role in a struggle that will not see its end for perhaps a billion years more.

There is a chance that the fabric of time itself can stand only a certain amount of change. After that point, it is possible that all existence could be obliterated—apparently Leiber's metaphor for a nuclear war on Earth. In the constant string of mankind's wars there has always been a winner and a loser, but now a nuclear war could effectively end all civilization and could result in the total destruction of human life through pestilence, radiation, and starvation.

The compactly written dialogue and the economical use of physical description in this 129-page novel mirror that of a short story, but the plot is developed to full-novel length. The characters seem to have a life of their own outside the book, coming or going from the Place. This effect is difficult to achieve in its comparatively brief length. The locked-room mystery and time-bomb suspense add intensity to the book and help make it a successful piece of writing.

In *The Big Time,* as elsewhere, Leiber is concerned with the value of the individual within a larger context. The Snakes and Spiders strive toward goals which will make their side predominant in the distant future. But the single agent sent back in time to carry out a mission cannot grasp the potential effects of his actions. A bomb exploded in ancient Greece during a major battle could slow down Greek expansion by years. This could lead to a chain reaction of events that might result in less power for the Greeks and a diminished significance of their impact upon the world's cultures. All the agent could experience, however, was the sight of thousands of Greeks being killed in an unfair battle due to outside intervention.

An analogy presents itself. One problem faced by modern manufacturing workers has been their feeling of isolation from the final results of their efforts. One craftsman used to carry out all phases of production of a cabinet, for example; cutting the wood, finishing it, joining it, and selling the cabinet to another person. The pride in good workmanship made up for the fatiguing labor. One could feel proud of the buyer's praise in a way that a person who only did one part of the job could not. Workers who run machines that cut boards into patterns have no contact with those who package the finished cabinets, and neither sees the sales staff as it discusses the product with buyers for a department store chain, let alone the consumer who purchases a piece of furniture.

The Leiber characters are not even sure that their actions have long-range good effects. Some of their missions are countered a few years later by opposing agents. Feeling cut off from the end products of their work, they are unenthused at the prospect of spending many years at it. The current term "burnout" applies to Greta, whose loved ones are gone and whose culture no longer exists in the way she knew it. Her excitement does not come from her work at the Place but from her romance with Erich, and even this is diminished by the possibility of his death at any moment during a foray into the past.

The Change War is being fought on billions of planets in millions of galaxies, under the overall direction of masters who are never actually seen by Snakes or Spiders, except for a few high-ranking ones. No one in *The Big Time* is certain what the masters even look like, although they are apparently some sort of evolved human or alien life form. The very scope of the battles, fought on so many planets and carried on at points quite remote in time from any individual's vantage point, inspires feelings of alienation and insignificance. Like the average people caught up in the events in *The Wanderer* and the meekly conforming masses in *The Sinful Ones*, the characters in *The Big Time* can never confront the greater world around them and bend it to their own will. They can improve their own lives and work with their friends and lovers to make life bearable, occasionally triumphing on a small scale.

"No Great Magic" presents a situation involving the theater, with some characters from *The Big Time*. Greta Forzane works for a theatrical company that is presenting *Macbeth* as a New York Theater in the Park performance. Greta has had amnesia and is trying to recover her memory as the performance begins. Step by step, her awareness grows until she sees that the theater is actually a part of the Change War, and that a skirmish between the Snakes and the Spiders is the reason behind the play.

Leiber sums up his view of the theater through Greta:

> . . . .If you wanted to time-travel and, well, do things, you could hardly pick a more practical machine than a dressing room and a sort of stage and half-theater attached, with actors to man it. Actors can fit in anywhere. They're used to learning new parts and wearing stage

> costumes. Heck, they're even used to traveling a lot. And if an actor's a bit strange, nobody thinks anything of it—he's almost expected to be foreign, it's an asset to him. . . . And theaters attract important people, the sort of people you might want to do something to. Caesar was stabbed in a theater. Lincoln was shot in one.

As wardrobe mistress, Greta learns more and more about the plot as it unfolds. An actress is to be substituted for the genuine Queen Elizabeth I—the theater itself has been transported to Elizabethan England. Greta notices this because the audience seems oddly dressed; she is living in the past with the theater troupe. This brings her out of her amnesia. As her memory returns, she recalls the manner of her lover Erich's death, a memory she had blocked out. "No Great Magic" effectively combines time travel and the theater and expresses Leiber's views about the power of the theater to let us travel in time.

The writer's lifelong interest in chess is shown in several short stories, including "The 64 Square Madhouse." In "Knight to Move," Erich von Hohenwald from *The Big Time* is present at a chess tournament on a planet of the star 61 Cygni in 5037 A.D., old Earth time. During the course of the match, it is suggested that Spider agents colonized the planets where chess is played because the knight chess piece has eight "crooked moves" that resemble the legs of a spider. (The piece can move ahead and to the side in what appear to be crooked directions rather than straight lines.) The Spiders' counterparts, the Snakes, might have originated dice games, since terms such as "snake eyes" refer to these.

The story features a minor confrontation between Erich and the Snake agent Erica Weaver, who both show up at the tournament among the thousand aliens competing or watching.

"A Deskful of Girls" has "Ghostgirls" similar to those in *The Big Time*, except that in this version they have a supernatural origin similar to the anima in Carl Jung's theories. In this story, a psychiatrist has captured living women and turned them into ectoplasmic shells of themselves. In the end, they seek revenge against him.

"The Haunted Future" takes a look at the future of Earth. Mental problems begin to increase among the residents of suburbs such as Civil Service Knolls. Judistrator Wisant and Securitor Harker consider themselves "sanitary engineers of the mind" who "hose out mental garbage." The story deals with loss of identity and individuality in cities and towns where the pressure to conform is strong. Then Individuality Unlimited begins selling its ideas on being different; "Soft-sell your superiority" and "accent the monster in you" are among its slogans. Wisant tells the cynical Dr. Snowden, "Most men are simply not equipped to use all the freedoms theoretically available to them." He thinks the upswing of insanity and neurosis comes from the impulses suppressed through the desire to conform. A rebel named Dave Cruxon challenges accepted behavior by disrupting a Tranquility Festival and creating mass hysteria. Characterizing the Age of Tranquility as the Age of Psychosis, he attempts to change the course of American life-styles. "The Haunted Future" once again shows Leiber's nonconformist views and sets up individualists who must battle against authority figures.

The Change War and *The Big Time* contributed a new version of time travel to the worlds of science fiction. No longer were time travelers on their way to the joys or wonders of the future. The future and the present became ambiguous and Leiber showed ambivalence about time travel. His protagonists must deal with the underlying purpose of the Change War and they do not enjoy being pawns in a much larger struggle than they will ever understand. The darker aspects of their activities, such as the kidnapping of the infant Einstein, apply to both sides.

Leiber took conventional science-fiction time travel and turned it inside out. Each wonder of the future or travel to the past has its price, and even immortality is an unhappy development because the immortals are soldiers in the war. They have immortality without personal freedom or a reason to go on living.

"Catch That Zeppelin!" won the Nebula Award as well as the Hugo Award for best SF short story of the year. First published in 1975, it takes an entirely different tack from the Change War stories. Rather than being a strong, resisting force, time is now greatly affected by small actions.

The narrator is Adolf Hitler, now transformed into a harmless gentleman, a businessman in an alternate world. World War I ended without the deep resentment of the German people that Hitler exploited in a second world war. Marie Sklodowska did not marry Pierre Curie to become Madame Curie; she married Thomas Edison and combined her experiments with his, developing a battery that made gasoline automobile engines unnecessary. Airships are safely powered by helium and no propeller aircraft are used, removing these two major sources of air pollution. The world is a much more peaceful place, where Germans were not exhorted by Hitler to kill Jews and where the underlying causes of World War II never materialized.

On a trip to meet his son in New York, Adolf finds himself caught in a sudden time warp. The time warp takes him into the world we know as real. Instead of the helium airship *Ostwald* moored at the top of the Empire State Building, awaiting passengers, there is now a World Trade Center, a world which has known World War II, depleted natural resources, pollution of air and water, and much suffering. The man finds that his counterpart led the world into a war in the 1930s.

As a result of the time warp, the man is now Fritz, about to meet his son Justin in New York. No longer at the "time cusp" that took him from one world to an alternate one, he cannot board the dirigible *Ostwald*—his ticket has vanished from his pocket. History now records that airships were filled with hydrogen and that one called the *Hindenberg* was destroyed in New Jersey in a fiery crash. Airships did not develop after that; they were replaced by propeller airplanes. The peaceful world no longer exists.

This story suggests that our lives have a certain fragility when viewed within the context of history. Certain key actions could have created an alternate world. Hitler might not have been warlike and internal combustion engines might not have revolutionized industry. Circumstances made Hitler into a dictator who could lead a nation into a war of revenge against the Allies, but events could just as easily have led to a different aftermath to World War I. Another Earth might have existed. SF writers have often dealt with alternate worlds and Leiber used this story and its "time cusps" to show how things could have worked out in a better way. One could take this as a warning story in the sense of H. G. Wells's *The Time Machine,* with our present trends leading us into an unhappy future. Like Wells's Time Traveler, we know that a multitude of current events add up to a future, and that changes today can divert the probable future from its path toward an unhappy end. On a different tack from his Change War stories, Leiber showed another view of how present actions can alter the future.

Destiny Times Three is not about time travel so much as possible alternate worlds, in a manner similar to that found in "Catch That Zeppelin!" No one can say for sure how the world would have turned out if certain different paths had been taken—such as a different outcome in an election, if an assassination had never happened, or had a country's leaders refrained from entering a war at a given time in history. *Destiny Times Three* is about alternate paths; significantly, Leiber wrote it during World War II.

In Norse mythology, the Yggdrasill was a huge ash tree whose branches extended into heaven and whose roots penetrated the underworld. Although various sources disagree as to the details of the myth, they concur that the tree symbolizes all existence. The word "Yggdrasill" means "the bearer of Odin"—Odin was the chief god in Norse mythology—and the Yggdrasill symbolizes the gallows on which Odin was hanged for nine days.

Leiber's inspiration for *Destiny Times Three* was this Norse legend. Originally titled *Roots of Yggdrasill,* he wrote the tale as a metaphorical version of the Norse legend of the three worlds, that of the gods, the frost giants, and of man. He envisioned his novel as "my masterpiece. . . a big canvas to fit a big subject."

The big novel was not to be, however. The magazine *Astounding Stories* would only serialize it if it were cut down substantially so that American servicemen would not miss parts of the story when wartime issues were delayed. Leiber hated to reduce it to two parts, but he did so. He later recalled that because of the nature of his novel, each character had to exist in triplicate; cutting down the bulk of the text meant taking out all the female characters (since they were slightly less important to the basic thread of the story):

> A drastic simplification to a manageable six [characters] was required, though I'm sure now it was a mistake to sacrifice the women. As a result, the novel has a ghostly, cold, lonely quality to me, peopled by the resentful, unseen female presences of all those cut characters. I don't think my Anima ever forgave me. . . . For the next five years I had a lot of trouble writing anything at all. My vengeful Anima, perhaps.

The above demonstrates that Leiber was conscious of female characters, unlike many SF writers who either decorated their male adventure stories with a few unimportant women or left them out without a thought. The anima the writer refers to is Carl Jung's term for the female impulse in the unconscious of a man, a concept important to the understanding of several of Leiber's works.

In its published final form as the novel *Destiny Times Three* (1945), the book centered around three major worlds, each an alternate to the others. In a rather confusing manner, Leiber introduces each alternate world and then reintroduces them at various points in the text. In order to simplify the complex story line for the reader, he arbitrarily gives the names World I, World II, and World III to these places. Characters from the three worlds, each of whom has the same name as his counterparts, are named Clawly I, Clawly II, Clawly III, and so on. As the differing characters and backgrounds unfold, the reader has to work to decipher them.

The tale begins with a play presenting the story of the "tree of life, with its roots in heaven and hell and the land of the frost giants, and serpents gnawing at those roots and the gods fighting to preserve it." This story is presented to an audience in an auditorium in an advanced type of world and is especially interesting to two men, since it reminds them of a theory they intend to discuss. Clawly is a small, dapper, lithe, and alert man with red hair, "like a devil-may-care Satan, harnessed for good purposes." His friend Thorn looks like "a somewhat disheveled and reckless saint, lured by evil." He is tall, gaunt, and resembles Leonardo da Vinci.

In the Sky Room of the Opal Cross—the single-building cities of this world are named after their outward forms and colors—Clawly and Thorn address the World Executive Council on a matter of great urgency. The two display an electronic map on which statistical symbols are plotted for the number of people in the population experiencing various symptoms. The number of people reporting severe nightmares that awaken them, and the number of people who experience "cryptic amnesia" seem to be rising. Cryptic amnesia occurs when people try to cover up their failure to recognize the members of their own family, a failure some are unable to hide.

On a map with colored lights representing each phenomenon, Clawly tries to demonstrate that symptoms are increasing rapidly. He theorizes that inhabitants of an alternate world, or else an alien force from another dimension, are infiltrating the Earth, and that alien minds are taking the place of Earth peoples' minds.

Unfortunately, Conjerly and the others in the Council denounce Clawly's ideas as superstitious. Every member of the Council turns against him, except one named Firemoor. Even his friend Thorn walks out on him.

Consulting in supposed secrecy with a mysterious seer named Oktav, Clawly is warned that the invasion is coming and that it is real. But Thorn sees the two of them together and notices that Oktav has left a small sphere behind. Unnoticed, Thorn picks it up. He has been seeing illusions of a face very much like his own, except pale and wraithlike, almost as if his mind were being taken over. The lost object, a talisman, sets the stage for a change in his existence.

In The Zone, a region outside normal space and time, Oktav meets with people who have access to the Probability Engine, a device that allows alternate worlds to be set up or destroyed. In this way, the implications of social and political changes can be viewed through these test results in laboratory worlds. But the main world is under the control of leaders who believe they know what is best for everyone and resist change.

By narrowing the "cone of possibilities" in a given world, however, the Probability Engine creates a new one. Key thoughts are placed in the minds of important people to influence their subsequent actions. The effects of these decisions and actions make for a vastly different world after a short time. The resulting civilizations do not know they are merely part of a test. Since a talisman permits the transfer of a mind to another body in such a world, Thorn could use it for that purpose and uncover the secrets of the Probability Engine. A man named Prim reminds Oktav that the lost talisman is Oktav's responsibility and that Thorn must not be allowed to use it to learn of the existence of alternate worlds.

The owners of the Probability Engine believe they are creating a laboratory for life and then justifiably destroying the life forms each time the world doesn't work out well. Oktav charges that this is like drowning unwanted kittens and then lavishing attention on one survivor. He contends that these are not really destroyed, but continue to exist as "botched worlds," where the unfortunate inhabitants must struggle to survive.

Duplicate worlds remain close to the main world at first and are the least different from that world. After a few months or years, the duplicates change in fundamental ways. In the first world, for example, the discovery and control of a plentiful source of energy, called subtronic power, produced a utopia. In World II, a small ruling elite controls access to subtronic power and does not share it, while a primitive and barbaric World III exists in which it has never been introduced. In all three cases the presence or absence of the power has greatly affected the development of civilization.

Meanwhile, mind transfers have been taking place. When the mind of one Thorn version is exchanged with that of another Thorn (Thorn I for Thorn II), each alienated man feels as though the people in the new world are acting in some kind of play. Clawly overhears that in this world people are being drafted into the military and that one unguarded reply to a government questioner can lead to induction. This tells him he is now in another world. Recalcitrants—those who oppose the government—are being sought out and captured. Thorn and Clawly separately decide that mind transfers must be taking place and that they must somehow find a way back to their own worlds.

On another level, Conjerly II has been one of the World II rulers planning a full-scale invasion of World I. Through a mind link that allows transfers to take place, they are preparing to invade in three days. Through infiltration, his world's invaders will prevent the World Executive Committee from taking any action against them in World I. Then Thorn I discovers what will allow a mind transfer: the fear of death. In the interim, he is thrust into another world, World III, of cave dwellers and wild animals. His body is now scarred, his hands have callouses and frostbite scars, and he is inhabiting Thorn III's body.

In order to warn the World I inhabitants of the invasion, having failed to convince them to take action, Clawly I takes Oktav's advice and creates a believable hoax of an upcoming invasion from Mars in three days. He plots out spurious warship movements and makes up Martian battle deployments.

Clawly's invasion hoax is discovered and preparedness for war relaxed just as the true invasion begins. The invasion forces arrive through the trans-time bridgehead which corresponds to the position of the World I Council chambers. Then the True Owners of the Probability Engine enter the tale. Although the leaders in World I have claimed they invented the Probability Engine, in reality they only found it. The True Owners, godlike aliens whose nature is never revealed, left it for them to find. The True Owners stop the invasion and tell their story.

Although they have permitted the thinking beings (the humans) to continue to use the Probability Engine, they have felt misgivings about permitting people on the botched worlds to come into existence, only to live in terrible conditions. Free will is allowed, however, to the point where the aliens decide to draw the line. The original purpose of the Engine was to test out social and political decisions, thereby preventing bad ones. Rather than destroy life after it was created, the aliens decide that the misuse of the Engine should go unpunished and that the people should be allowed to live.

In a happy ending, all three Clawly versions are allowed to cross-pollinate their thoughts by combining their minds, and the three versions are given existence on a higher plane of thought, following which they are sent back to their three worlds. The improvement of life by the introduction of subtronic power will enhance World III's people's lives, and the overturn of World II's tyrannical leaders will improve the quality of life there as well.

Destiny Times Three ends with the aliens telling the humans, "We will watch your future with interest, hoping someday to welcome you into the commonwealth of mature beings." Clawly will now alternate one week each in each of the three worlds.

Destiny Times Three is a science-fiction novel with the elements common to many *Astounding Stories* tales. Rather than an occult or fantasy explanation for all wonders, there is a scientific rationale. The characters are thrust into danger and must escape it without resorting to magic. Invasion themes in SF were understandably prevalent in the wake of the world wars. Allegorical allusions to the Germans or Japanese cropped up frequently in invasion stories during this period. While Leiber never wrote one of the so-called yellow peril stories as so many others in the SF and non-SF pulp magazines did, *Destiny Times Three* is at least an invasion story.

This novel is less satisfying than many of Leiber's works. Perhaps this is because he originally conceived of it as a large, complex novel, but even in its final, pared-down form it is often confusing. The three different worlds are hard to follow, and in a larger novel they might have been even more perplexing. It is difficult to understand enough to understand one world in a complicated work of science fiction (past, future, catlike aliens, reptile cultures, and so on) without having to grapple with two more of them in alternating chapters or even within chapters. Here is an example:

> He wondered what was happening to those other Thorns, in their hodgepodged destinies. Thorn III in World II—had he died in the instant of arrival there, or had the Servants noted the personality-change in time and perhaps spared him? Thorn II in World I. Thorn I in World III. It was like some crazy game—some game devised by a mad, cruel god.

In order to clear up this confusion, Leiber provides plot summaries at a number of places in the book. He succeeds in tying up some of the loose ends, but only at the cost of dry writing. Speeches between two people who already know what each is talking about (and are thus conversing only to let the reader overhear) are common in science fiction, but rather rare in Fritz Leiber. Unfortunately, they occur in this novel.

The ending of *Destiny Times Three* is a deus ex machina. From out of nowhere, the space aliens decide to change the outcome of the events. The best science fiction novels do not have this element, which nullifies all that has gone on before. The "cavalry" coming to the rescue is the type of stopgap ending found in the worst science-fiction stories and novels since the early 1900s. Heartwarming but cheaply-won happy endings seldom satisfy. Although *Destiny Times Three* contains adventure, colorful settings, and interesting characters, it does not represent one of Leiber's best works.

5

Sword-and-Sorcery:
Fafhrd and the Gray Mouser

Heroic fantasy is a much-maligned category of writing that falls somewhere within the genre of fantasy or sometimes science fiction, depending upon the story. Those who strictly define the term science fiction would usually place heroic fantasy outside the genre.

Another term for heroic fantasy is "sword-and-sorcery." Leiber was the originator of this widely-used term, which describes the type of story written by Robert E. Howard in his popular Conan the Barbarian series. A heroic barbarian swordsman or hand-combat fighter battles against witchcraft or sorcery in most such tales. The hero fights illusion, dreams, apparitions, ghosts, and other dangers by sword, dagger, or brute strength.

Sword-and-sorcery has been most popular with young men between their early teens and late twenties. This is not to say that others do not enjoy the genre, but its wish-fulfillment aspects appeal most strongly to young men. Their self-images are threatened by potential rejection by women, failure at their jobs, or physical harm by other men. They feel better when they read about a strong, fearless man, a hero with whom they can identify, whose fictional exploits can become theirs in fantasy for a few hours of reading. This is part of the appeal of James Bond, Western heroes, and the film appearances of John Wayne. Not all young men read sword-and-sorcery, of course, while young women, for whom romance novels sometimes serve their wish-fulfillment purposes (according to some observers), are beginning to have more interest in it. Jessica Amanda Salmonson's series of anthologies featuring strong women as heroes, *Amazons!* (1979), helped start a trend of nonsexist examples of the genre.

The chief exponents of sword-and-sorcery include Lin Carter, L. Sprague de Camp, Andrew Offutt, Gardner Fox, Tanith Lee, C. L. Moore, Robert E. Howard, and Fritz Leiber, plus a handful of others. Howard was the giant in the field, and his Conan and Kull books are still selling after more than four decades, with total sales in the tens of millions.

The drawbacks of most heroic fantasy are many. The stories tend to follow a formula. A brawny, muscular, and usually oafish barbarian battles against the odds and wins. He shows little respect for women as equals, regarding them as decorative ornaments or objects to be used for a brief time and then quickly forgotten. Few ongoing relationships with women exist in such tales. The hero fights his way out of difficulty, and the reader knows he will win in the end. There is little real danger, since the hero always returns in a sequel. For these reasons, many people give up on the genre after one or two books.

Fritz Leiber's sword-and-sorcery is an exception. It centers around two men named Fafhrd and the Gray Mouser, whom Leiber once described this way:

> Fafhrd and Mouser are rogues through and through, though each has in him a lot of humanity and at least a diamond chip of the spirit of true adventure. They drink, they feast, they wench, they brawl, they steal, they gamble, and surely they hire out their swords to powers that are only a shade better, if that, than the villains. . . . One of the original motives for conceiving Fafhrd and the Mouser was to have a couple of fantasy heroes closer to true human stature than supermen like Conan and Tarzan and many another. . . . they're rogues in a decadent world where you have to be a rogue to survive.

Leiber recalled that the two heroes were conceived during the Depression and did not appear in print for five years. He had been exchanging voluminous letters, sometimes ten pages in length, with his friend Harry Otto Fischer, often involving imaginary situations and characters. Fischer's knowledge of legend, myth, and history, combined with Leiber's readings and theatrical background, led Fischer to suggest, in September 1934, the idea of the two of them writing about heroes Fischer had thought up.

> For all do fear the one known as the Gray Mouser. He walks with swagger 'mongst the bravos, though he's but the stature of a child. His costume is all of gray, from gauntlets to boots and spurs of steel. His flat, swart face is shadowed by a peaked cap of mouse-skin and his garments are of silk, strangely soft and coarse of weave. His weapons: one called Cat's Claw, for it kills in the dark unerringly, and his longer sword, curved up, he terms the Scalpel, for it lets the heart's blood as neatly as a surgeon.

His companion Fafhrd was described as a man seven feet in height:

> His light chestnut hair was bound in a ringlet of pure gold, engraved with runes. His eyes, wide-set, were proud and of fearless mien. His wrist between gauntlet and mail was white as milk and thick as a hero's ankle. His features were lean cut and his mouth smiled as he fingered the ponderous hilt of a huge longsword with long and nimble fingers.

But neither Leiber nor Fischer took the time to work out all the details until Leiber did so, when he first imagined a creature holding eight swords in as many arms, fighting the Mouser. This has expanded to encompass the exploits of Fafhrd and the Gray Mouser in short stories, novellas, and one full-length novel, gathered into a six-volume set.

The first publication of the tales was in science-fiction magazines such as *Unknown* and *Fantastic Stories*. Sometimes Leiber wrote new material with background information that filled in the spaces between two chronologically separate stories or that set the mood for the following tale. Some stories take place during the time before the two characters met, others depict their youth, some portray them at the peak of their powers, and still others deal with their old age. This is quite rare in SF and fantasy, where heroes usually stay young forever. Leiber's allowing for aging and a slowing down of physical prowess is more sophisticated and natural.

Part of the charm of the Leiber stories is in their bantering and humor. Ursula K. LeGuin contended in an essay that Leiber and

Roger Zelazny (who writes the popular Amber series of sword-and-sorcery) seemed willing to poke fun at their own stories:

> . . . it is perfectly clear that Leiber, profoundly acquainted with Shakespeare and practiced in a very broad range of techniques, could maintain any tone with eloquence and grace. Sometimes I wonder if these two writers underestimate their own talents, if they lack confidence in themselves. Or it may be that, since fantasy is seldom taken seriously at this particular era in this country, they are afraid to take it seriously. They don't want to be caught believing in their own creations, getting all worked up about imaginary things; and so their humor becomes self-mocking, self-destructive. Their gods and heroes keep turning aside to look out of the book at you and whisper, "See, we're really just plain folks."

Not all the stories involve humor or satire. Most take place in an atmosphere of melancholy or introspection. Similar to the sword-and-sorcery books of English author Michael Moorcock (which include *The Eternal Champion, The Silver Warriors,* and the popular and highly-praised Elric, Hawkmoon, and Corum books), Leiber's stories reflect a sense of futility regarding the ultimate "victory" of the combatants. In the majority of fantasy quest novels (as written by Tolkien, for example), the heroes battle against odds and reach a happy ending, having realized their main goals. We assume the future is bright. Moorcock's and Leiber's series have heroes winning temporary victories and short-term goals within a limited area, but we feel that no victory is permanent, and more challenges await them. Moorcock's heroes battle against some small segment of a larger group of villains, sometimes including a death and rebirth as a different hero in a seemingly unending struggle. Leiber's heroes seem content with the idea that they will never achieve true happiness, but they still keep seeking it.

Leiber's heroes are not invincible brutes. They sometimes win and sometime lose, unlike most other heroes. There have been tragic losses for both men, including their freedom. The women they dearly loved early in the saga were taken from them, leaving them lonely and unhappy.

The gods of Nehwon (which is "Nowhen" read backwards) are

capricious and utterly unreliable, often acting on sudden whims. Leiber might have created the gods in this fashion because our own world seems to be ruled over by a God who sometimes aids us by a miracle, but at other times leaves us to suffer while a demonstrably evil crime syndicate boss leads a long life of luxury. As *Gather, Darkness!* showed, Leiber has a cynical view of the theology behind organized religion.

The gods in some fantasy books act as fairy godmothers or benevolent and fatherly wizards, always ready with a chant or a rune to ward off evil. The Leiber gods do not always answer Fafhrd and Mouser's chants, and the amulets and charms given to the two men very often are worthless. Only the intelligence, fighting prowess, and luck of the two heroes win the day for them in most stories.

There isn't room here to analyze or examine the complete contents of the six volumes of prose about Fafhrd and the Gray Mouser. However, we can take a brief tour of their world, stopping along the way to discuss points of interest.

The first volume is called *Swords and Deviltry* and it contains three tales: "The Snow Women" (1970), "The Unholy Grail" (1962), and "Ill Met in Lankhmar" (1970). "The Snow Women" is set in the time before Fafhrd met his companion. Fafhrd's mother, jealous that her son has fallen in love with a young woman from a land to the south, opposes his forthcoming marriage to her. North country women control their men, no matter how strong and barbaric: "Each Snow Woman, usually with the aid of the rest, worked to maintain absolute control of her man, though leaving him seemingly free." Fafhrd's mother "believes that both pleasure and rest were bad for men."

Fafhrd's interest in Vlana, a young woman from a touring theatrical troupe, rouses the jealousy of the local women, among them Mara, who has had no opportunity within the northern culture of Cold Corner for training in dancing and no place to wear fine clothes. The young Mara decides that "Vlana ought to be whipped out of Cold Corner, and Fafhrd needed a woman to run his life and keep his mad imagination in check. Not his mother, of course—that awful and incestuous eater of her own son—but a glamorous and shrewd young wife. Herself."

The implied witchcraft becomes explicitly real since the northern women use their ice magic to fight the visiting southern women's powers of fire. Fafhrd knows that his mother, Mor, had the power and will to murder Fafhrd's father. She wanted to punish his father for disobeying her orders when he went mountain climbing, and by means of a spell, she made him fall to his death. Men know that women have these powers, and sometimes speculate about whether or not some current ill effect is the cause of a woman's evil magic.

Mor's most significant contribution to the series of stories comes when she casts a powerful spell against her son Fafhrd which will make his heart cold forever. This means he will ache with need for a woman's love, but will always lack the emotional satisfaction of it. As Fafhrd attempts to leave the Snow Tribe to live an independent life with Vlana, his mother unleashes agents of death to kill both of them, rather than see them happy and free. Fafhrd remarks: "Women are horrible. I mean, quite as horrible as men. Oh, is there anyone in the wide world that has aught but ice water in his or her veins?"

Unlike his father, the two are able to escape. They seek "travel, love, adventure, the world!" Following Fafhrd always, however, will be his mother's curse: "There is a witchy cold that can follow you anywhere in Nehwon. Wherever ice once went, witchery can send it again."

While Leiber was exploring his ambivalent feelings toward women, he was also providing a new twist on an old theme. Relationships between men and women are rarely egalitarian in fantasy or science-fiction stories. Early SF had few worthwhile female characters and almost no well-rounded and mature male ones. Later stories, including those by feminist women, have dealt with a mixture of types, but most were in obvious reaction to the earlier ones. Instead of an unintelligent, decorative woman who faints on the arm of the officer who has killed an alien creature with a single blaster shot, we now generally find strong-willed, powerful women who do not need men in their lives, or who use them as sex objects. Such simple role reversals do not make the best characterizations either, but perhaps this should be expected during a transitional period as feminism gains greater acceptance. As far as Leiber was concerned, he wrote the Fafhrd and Gray Mouser stories over many years, and he gradually modified his style of handling male and female characters.

A case in point is "Under the Thumbs of the Gods," in which women are strong, independent, and sympathetically presented. Each time the two men try to assert themselves romantically, the women reject them, because of their past record. The women object to the way they have been used, and the men's macho attitudes are going to have to change, because everywhere they go, women are behaving differently and expecting respect. Although women are still powerful in this story, they are not villains.

Vlana and the other women are presented sympathetically in several other stories. In *Swords against Wizardry*, Leiber even refers to Alyx the Picklock, a strong heroine created by feminist writer Joanna Russ (who enjoys his books in this genre).

The first meeting of Fafhrd and the Gray Mouser is described in "Ill Met in Lankhmar," which won the Hugo Award for the Best Novella of the Year (1970). The story tells of the assault on the local Thieves' House (headquarters for the trade union of robbers and burglars known as the Thieves' Guild). Fafhrd has had a grudge against the Guild because Vlana had one, and this leads to conflict. The colorful background of Lankhmar, the city where many of the stories are set, features such avenues as Death Alley, Cash Street, Whore Street, Pimp Street, Street of the Thinkers (called Atheist Avenue by moralists), Cheap Street, and Crafts Street. The Temple of the Gods of Lankhmar is east of town and the marshes are to the west.

In "Lean Times in Lankhmar" there is religious satire, as Fafhrd becomes a devotee of the minor god Issek of the Jug and tries to convert everyone else to follow him under the religion of "Issekianity." The "has-been god" Issek has wanted to make a comeback after being imprisoned in a jug for seventeen years. Fafhrd even shaves his head and becomes religious in sympathy. The Gray Mouser, meanwhile, has parted company with his friend and has hired himself out as a member of an organized crime protection racket, assigned to intimidate the religious figures who inhabit the Street of the Gods.

Whether following their patron wizards Sheelba of the Eyeless

Face (the Mouser's mentor), and Ningauble of the Seven Eyes (Fafhrd's wizard), or striking out on their own, the two encounter more than their share of barbarian sword-wielders, shadowy ghosts, and demons. By the sixth volume, Leiber has allowed the two men to age somewhat and to change with experience.

Along with coining the term "sword-and-sorcery," Leiber's contribution to the genre consists mainly of his deviation from the previous Robert E. Howard style of barbarian strongman hero. His two heroes complement each other and develop a compassionate friendship, which grows over time. Thanks partly to Leiber's influence, sword-and-sorcery has become more sophisticated and wide-ranging than a few years ago. The greatest compliment he has received for it has been when people tell him that they ordinarily disdain the genre but read and enjoy his tales.

In the late 1970s a game called Lankhmar was sold by the company TSR. This was an authorized version of the board game that Fischer and Leiber had devised many years earlier, similar to Dungeons and Dragons. Using a rule booklet written by the two authors, the game has familiar characters and scenes taken directly from the Fafhrd and Gray Mouser books, with pieces moved on the Lankhmar board.

6

Creatures of Darkness: Horror

Fritz Leiber's ideas about supernatural horror fiction were partly shaped by his readings and personal taste, but the influence of Howard Phillips Lovecraft (1890–1937) was of major importance. Lovecraft's books dealt mainly with the macabre, whether in stories about ancient curses later fulfilled, legends from the past that haunt the present, or various menacing creatures that enter the environs of a small town in New England.

Leiber married Jonquil Stephens in 1936, and she knew of her husband's interest in Lovecraft's writings. Jonquil wrote to Lovecraft and this encouraged the two men to enter into a correspondence that lasted the few remaining months of Lovecraft's life. Leiber recalled the influence of those letters:

> That spring we'd driven out to Beverly Hills, California, and were temporarily living with my actor father and mother. I was supposed to be trying to get a job in the movies, but really I was trying unsuccessfully to write something—anything—for the magazine *Weird Tales*. That brief but intense and *industrious* contact with a professional writer of weird stories strengthened in me a realization of the worth of the cosmic weird tale, the serious supernatural horror story, and set me an example of honesty, scholarship, and care in writing which has by fits and starts stuck with me.

Leiber continued writing for publication, in part thanks to the encouragement of Lovecraft, who spread news of the arrival of "young Leiber" among the established horror writers such as Robert

Bloch, Frank Belknap Long, and Clark Ashton Smith. Leiber was at a crossroads in his life, and his decision to stay with horror writing (and submission to magazines in the field) was a crucial one for his career.

Leiber has often pointed to one particular passage in Lovecraft's book *Supernatural Horror in Literature* as being one with which he agrees:

> The one test of the really weird is simply this—whether or not there be excited in the reader a profound sense of dread, and of contact with the unknown spheres and powers; a subtle attitude of awed listening, as if for the beating of black wings or the searching of outside shapes and entities on the known universe's utmost rim. And of course, the more completely and unifiedly a story conveys this atmosphere, the better it is as a work of art in the given medium.

Leiber was always conscious of this test for horror, as demonstrated by his stories and novels that show the "profound sense of dread," and the feeling of the unknown forces on the boundaries of the rational and known.

He seems to have been spurred to consciously write in a serious manner and to explore the plausible aspects of the unknown. The worst of the horror fiction he read was written by people who did not truly care about the genre. What Lovecraft had called "shoddy" writing appearing in "pulp rags" had brought the field down to a level unappealing to fantasy writers, except for those who could see beyond the limits imposed upon horror fiction by commercial constraints.

Leiber saw in Lord Dunsany's and Edgar Allan Poe's works the sort of literary horror he wanted to write. Lovecraft's statement about a unified weird tale that focused upon the genuine unknown—as opposed to the ludicrous and unimaginative monster stories by hacks—was a distillation of the thinking Lovecraft had done over the years and of his voluminous correspondence with his friends.

When Leiber wrote *Conjure Wife, Our Lady of Darkness,* and many of his short stories, he chose to deal with the unknown forces present at the outside boundaries of scientific knowledge. The dread in contacting the "unknown spheres and powers" comes partly from the nature of these forces, and partly from the act of leaving behind the comforting certainties of civilized man—certainties that have proven unreliable when pitted against witchcraft (*Conjure Wife*) or the forces unleashed by a cult leader's curse (*Our Lady of Darkness*). Smug confidence in one's sense of reality can be shattered quickly by occult forces, and this excites the "profound sense of dread" Leiber was able to produce in his horror fiction.

Leiber shared with Lovecraft a feel for the eerie aspects of the unknown in relation to established scientific theory, as expressed in this passage from Lovecraft's letter to Leiber dated November 18, 1936:

> In my view of the universe I probably side more—objectively and intellectually—with the material man of science than with the mystic; but my repudiation of unverified trimmings causes me to reject unjustified extrapolations and dogmata on one side as well as on the other . . . We don't know what we are in time and space, or what will happen to us before our kind of matter and energy will cease to exist. Organic life is only a momentary incident—whether a local and unique accident or a widespread cosmic principle often repeated, we can never know. We can never know how far our kind of natural law holds good in the gulfs of space and time, or when some manifestation of it will change.

Not only did he follow this principle in his horror stories, adding one element from outside the realm of the rational and the accepted, but also in *The Wanderer*. The civilizations of spacefaring emigrants in that book landed on one planet after another, altering existing physical properties (in using the matter of planets for fuel or breaking them up) and testing the limits of time and space. Tigerishka and the Wild Ones wanted to explore hyperspace and to satisfy their curiosity about what lay beyond the rim of the known universe.

Leiber was always skeptical in his assessment of the pseudoscience espoused by Velikovsky and others, as well as the writings of witchcraft devotees. Like Lovecraft, he sided with the findings of science over the theories of mysticism, but he gained some of the tension needed for suspenseful horror from the strain in the fabric of scientific knowledge when new, incongruous evidence threatens to tear it apart.

Norman Saylor, the protagonist of *Conjure Wife*, feels precisely this sense of doom when he notices what can only be the effects of true, working magic. But Norman does not accept this easily. He is a rational, civilized man—a sociology professor at the fictional Hempnell College—and not at all superstitious. With Norman, Leiber sets up the novel's main conflict: science versus the unexplained.

Conjure Wife first appeared in the April, 1943 issue of *Unknown Worlds*, edited by John W. Campbell, Jr. Leiber based his tale on his experience of the college atmosphere during his year as instructor. He had observed the pressure to conform within the college faculty, and the fierce infighting for tenure, prestige, and department chairmanships. He disliked the toadying and flattery by faculty wives at social gatherings, a part of the political battles fought beneath the calm exterior of small-college life.

The novel opens from that point of view, as Norman Saylor is about to look through his wife Tansy's dresser drawers. Although he suffers guilt for doing this, curiosity has gotten the better of him, and at the same time, he reflects on her ability to deal with life at Hempnell College. He decides that Hempnell tests a married couple's endurance, with its

> narrow unamiable culture with its taboos against mentioned reality, its elaborate suppression of sex, its insistence on a stoical ability to withstand a monotonous routine of business or drudgery—and in the midst, performing the necessary rituals to keep dead ideas alive, like a college of witch-doctors in their stern stone tents, powerful, property-owning Hempnell. . . . Tansy especially, he was sure, had at first found everything nerve-wracking.

In Tansy's dresser Saylor finds a box of graveyard dirt, fingernail parings, and snippings of hair, each item labeled with a person's name. Saylor has researched and written papers on Negro magic, the relationship between ancient superstition and modern neuroses, and the feminine element in superstition. Tansy has read these in progress and has gone with him on field trips. He concludes now that she has applied much more of the information than he imagined. As he opens one of her books and reads such marginal notes as, "Doesn't work. Substitute copper filings for brass. Try in dark moon instead of full," she suddenly comes into the room and sees him.

Leiber has now set the tone for the novel. *Conjure Wife* relentlessly probes the conflict between Norman's rationality and Tansy's belief in magic. She has apparently proven certain rituals effective, although Norman can argue that it was simply coincidence and that a world today has no need of unscientific explanations.

Norman has speculated about how he and Tansy fit into the hostile Hempnell life like "a young warrior and squaw who had blundered into a realm of ancestral ghosts and always managed to keep secret their true flesh-and-blood nature despite a thousand threatened disclosures, because Tansy happened to know the right protective charms."

The novel constantly reassesses the two positions, testing whether Tansy only imagines that magic works, or if Norman is incautiously ignoring it. The power of *Conjure Wife* lies in its careful groundwork of information, leading the reader to believe fully in witchcraft despite Norman's skepticism. The faculty wives at Hempnell are evil, despicable witches who have only been held at bay by Tansy's knowledge of protective charms and talismans. Norman has been reaping the benefits without realizing they came from Tansy's magic, without which his own talents and hard work would have been useless. The reader thus empathizes with Tansy in her attempts to understand herself, to discover whether she is becoming neurotic or not, and as she tries to convince Norman that evil forces are surrounding the two of them.

Although we are convinced that Tansy is right, we also consider the possibility that illusions cloud all her perceptions. If she is paranoid, she would not know it and thus might well think that witches' conspiracies cause all the evil around her. On the other hand, if she is not paranoid, then Norman is foolishly closing his mind to the real danger. Coincidence can be stretched in the service of rational logic, and Norman tries to stretch it as far as it will go.

At one point, after he has rather condescendingly tried to "help" Tansy by forcing her to leave behind all her protective charms and spells, a huge stone gargoyle is moved from a college building onto the front doorstep of the Saylor house. A witch's spell has done this; Norman even saw the stone bird in several different places on the roof. Nonetheless, he ignores all this and risks being crushed by the stone bird as it tries to get into his house. But his wife has returned to her old ways at the last minute and has knotted together a protective charm to keep out danger. The gargoyle crushes the Saylor cat to death and falls just short of getting into the house.

Norman is afraid, but still concludes that some college fraternity men must have somehow moved the stone bird onto their lawn, and that lightning happened to hit it just then. He has no explanation for how the giant stone creature could have been transported there, and dismisses the fact that earlier on he saw one of the faculty wives with a series of photos of the gargoyle. Norman's explanation does not satisfy the reader, who is fully persuaded that old-fashioned witchcraft exists.

One approach to writing horror stories (and film screenplays in the genre) is to maintain one character's haughty attitude about the nonsense that others are spouting concerning monsters, witchcraft, or ghosts. All the oddities, unlikely events, and cruel deaths in the book or film can be called coincidence, accident, or the work of criminals who took pains to cover their traces. Regardless of how pious and smug the local sheriff or acknowledged expert may be, the audience knows the werewolf or vampire really exists.

In horror films the audience believes in the existence of the supernatural menace, whereas in normal circumstances it would be strongly suspicious and skeptical of reports of living mummies or other monsters. The suspension of disbelief, a vital part of the work of a science-fiction or horror writer, is thus achieved. A person who would in real life laugh at a tabloid headline about werewolves or an abduction by a UFO alien can be won over in a well-written story of horror. The readers who begin by seeing themselves as Norman Saylor types (rational and logical doubters) are now converted, at least temporarily, into Tansy Saylor types (believers in the occult world of witchcraft).

Leiber's novel contains more elements than the bare bones of the horror plot. Norman is jealous of Tansy's occult practices, up to now a secret. His wife, whom he thought he knew intimately, has kept much from him. This is partly why he forces her to abandon witchcraft, but he is also trying to protect and reinforce his own opinions. He has felt rather smugly comfortable up to now in his beliefs.

There is always a chance, however, that any philosophy or religion can be shattered by a revelation of its weaknesses. If such a revelation could show basic flaws in science and its rational conclusions—not merely point out the absence of certain information—then the foundation of science, its very method, would be in jeopardy. Conditions in which gravity could be eliminated on Earth, in which E did not equal MC^2, or in which the velocity of light could be exceeded would disprove the theories scientists currently hold dear. Similarly, a totally nonscientific system of repeatable experimental results, such as working witchcraft, would actually be a new form of science. *Conjure Wife*'s witchcraft is imperfect, but one can see that increased knowledge and experimentation, along with records of results, could improve its effectiveness. And the Norman Saylors of this world would fear anything that challenged their own systems of assumptions about our environment and how it works.

Tansy needs to protect her husband. When Norman was nearly dying of pneumonia once, she reverted to some childhood rituals she hoped somehow would cure him. He was cured, and she couldn't help think that her rituals helped. One might say this could have been a reinforcement of a neurotic's obsessive-compulsive ritual behavior, or one might say this was an introduction to the reality of witchcraft.

Confused and uncertain, Tansy continues to test out some of the rituals she has learned during her ten years of marriage to a researcher in superstition. She discovers the methods of occult believers from around the world as her husband gathers research material, incorporates some into her own practices, and credits his career advancement to the performance of magic as much as to his abilities.

The turning point comes when Norman forces Tansy to find and destroy each charm and protective device and to give up witchcraft. The flannel packets hidden in clothing, the anchor and heart (for security) sewn into their feather pillows—everything must be destroyed. Although she feels better once the charms are gone, and Norman congratulates himself for helping her to help herself, she inadvertently has forgotten one last charm. Norman later finds it inside the photo compartment in a locket. He pries it open and tosses the last charm into the fireplace.

But as Tansy's protection ends, the ill effects follow immediately, explainable in Norman's mind as "unpleasant coincidences." The room seems to darken and the cat (still alive at that point) runs out, although Tansy is asleep and doesn't know what has happened. But the series of unhappy events continues. Norman receives a phone call from a hysterical student who has waited until that night to tell him he blames Norman for flunking him. The phone rings again, this time from a disturbed young woman who tells him she wants to become his mistress. He laughs at her, and she goes into a rage.

The following day, a faculty member warns Norman that a trustee is mad about a wild party the Saylors attended at which some theater people acted indecorously. The Dean of Women, the elderly Mrs. Carr, asks Norman, "And *how* is Tansy?" (which can now be interpreted to mean, "has anything bad happened to Tansy yet, now that her guard is down?"). Shortly afterwards, Norman is accused of plagiarizing a doctoral dissertation. If the accusation stands, Saylor will lose his job, and his reputation will be ruined in academia, making it nearly impossible for him to work in the field he loves. The flunked student again threatens him, and his would-be mistress seeks revenge by claiming that Norman has actually had an affair with her. Victim of a curse concerning sharp objects, Norman bleeds excessively when he cuts himself shaving and while handling a letter-opener. Then, at a card party attended by Mrs. Carr and two other antagonistic women, probably witches, Norman suspects evil intentions from all three. Faculty wives have been known to promote their husbands' careers, he recalls, and concludes that their hostility stems from this.

As worse and worse "luck" pursues Norman, he entertains thoughts of suicide, probably the consequence of a curse, but he doesn't know it—he is still struggling against the idea that Tansy's charms worked. The incident involving the stone gargoyle happens as his faith in rationality is failing, but nevertheless he feels that we have evolved beyond our primitive ancestors and must overcome their backward ideas through modern logic and knowledge.

During this time, he has kept most of his troubles a secret from Tansy. Once he tells her, however, she convinces him to repeat that all he has is hers, and we know this means she will now help him fight the evil summoned against him—personified as a huge, invisible creature stalking behind him.

The pressure and tension immediately drop away from Norman. Although he loses the department chairmanship he has sought, and undergoes heavy fire from several directions—in one case, literally, as the failed student tries to shoot him but misses—he now feels confident he can work out his problems, difficult as they are. Even the faculty rivalries seem manageable now.

Norman then finds a note and discovers that Tansy has taken on the burden of the deadly creature. She tells him the exact magic formula to use to rescue her. Although he resists using witchcraft, he fears she may lose her life or her soul, since one of the faculty witches now possesses Tansy's vital diary containing all of her chants and private personal information, making Tansy vulnerable to curses.

He finally uses the magic formula, but he finishes the procedures one minute too late. Tansy is thus condemned to a hellish existence: she loses her own soul to the seventy-year-old Mrs. Carr, who exchanges bodies with her. If Tansy tried to tell anyone what has happened, no one would believe her; they would think her a senile old woman.

But the ending never spells out whether everything could be explained without supernatural forces. Tansy now inhabits another woman's body, but she could also have exerted some sort of neurotic influence over the other woman, who herself, out of a delusion, could have taken on Tansy's characteristics. Norman might have been battling against three old women, potential psychotics, who only believed they were witches, and Tansy could have been in a temporary state of multiple-personality psychosis. However, we know the odds are against all this; witchcraft exists and had to be fought against.

Leiber has said he wrote *Conjure Wife* to carry further the theme of Sir James Barrie's play *What Every Woman Knows* (1908). In this play, women let men think it's a "man's world" but know that they themselves really rule. *Conjure Wife* would have us believe that all women possess the potential to use witchcraft for power. Not all women know this, and some only dabble in it, but others use this power regularly. In one scene, Tansy has lost her soul and summons a black maid to her hotel room at night. Answering Tansy's questions for Norman's benefit, the maid tells about learning rituals as a little girl, about trial-and-error attempts at casting spells, and her conclusion that some women are better at witchcraft than others.

This story reveals a fear of women. Whether it is Leiber's fear or not, it is impossible to say, but in the novel, a conspiracy of powerful women controls men's lives. This was also true in the Fafhrd and Gray Mouser story "The Snow Women," in which women like Fafhrd's mother were able to cast spells and subdue men's yearning for freedom and independence. When *Conjure Wife* was written in the early 1940s, women had fewer career opportunities open to them than today. Except for a few fields, there were almost no women professors or administrators at universities and colleges, and women were closed off in their attempts to gain direct power. To be the wife of an important male in academia might have had to substitute for a woman's real professional needs, as artificial and uninspiring as that compromise might have been. Thus, in any culture that denies women direct access to power, they may try to achieve it indirectly by manipulating others around them.

To attribute faculty-wife infighting to witchcraft is, of course, an excursion into pure fiction, but *Conjure Wife* extrapolates brilliantly on a man's fears of being manipulated by a woman. While the women's movement has won some gains in career choices and advancement for women, fear of women, especially in professional roles, remains a stumbling block. The so-called witches of earlier times were usually solitary old women who lived in unconventional ways. They did not marry, or were widows, and they did not have many friends. Cruel people made up stories about them, and superstition-fired legends grew about them being witches. Bad luck could thus be ascribed to these scapegoats. Whether in the Middle Ages or in a more recent century in Salem, Massachusetts, thousands of women have been unfairly accused of witchcraft. To fit the *Unknown Worlds* requirements, stories almost always supplied a plausible rationale for their seemingly supernatural events. *Conjure Wife* depicts magic which, if properly refined and rigorously tested, could be a new type of science. Repeated trials might not yield identical results, but only because of imperfect physical substances (such as impure metal filings), or a stronger counterspell, and so on, just as chemistry experiments would fail to verify previous findings if the strength and purity of their component chemicals were not identical. Folk medicines have sometimes been effective, despite incorrect assumptions by their users; aspirin was developed from tree bark, and a healing chemical was discovered in spider webs. Norman Saylor speculates that, like alchemists who made some discoveries by chance, modern witches could make more if they worked systematically. This attitude enhances the reader's suspension of disbelief much better than would a sudden revelation that magic works (as would happen in a fantasy novel).

Asked about the autobiographical elements in *Conjure Wife,* Leiber explained:

> Actually, it was based partly on my experience teaching speech and dramatics for one year at Occidental College in Los Angeles, at Eagle Rock. I taught there for the year 1941-1942, the same year as Pearl Harbor. My wife Jonquil was there with me and that sort of gave me the background of the two leading characters. I imagined myself farther along in my academic career and studying anthropology. It was the same kind of a small college. I'm pretty sure it was the same college Huxley used in his novel *After Many a Summer Dies the Swan,* although in the book he calls it Tarzana College.

According to Leiber's son, Justin, Jonquil had always read with fascination about witchcraft and the occult, while Fritz was skeptically interested in both subjects.

In *Conjure Wife,* he created a masterpiece of modern horror, satisfying the *Unknown Worlds* credibility requirements and at the same time rising above the typical horror novel of the time. Instead of setting it in a haunted house or a gloomy castle, Leiber chose a contemporary college town. Far ahead of his time with *Conjure Wife,* one of the first modern horror novels, Leiber departed from the stilted language of some of the genre's earlier writers and brought the characterization and writing style up to current standards for fiction. He makes us care about the Saylors so that we do not leaf idly through the pages, thinking that witchcraft is nonsense. As a result, his book stands up well alongside the fine work of the Stephen Kings and Peter Straubs of the '70s and early '80s.

Leiber achieves suspense and terror without a mass of gory deaths or bloody scenes. Only one death occurs, that of a cat, and the only flowing blood is Norman's, shed when he cuts himself a few times. The horror usually lies offstage, similar to the technique of old-time radio programs, and many would say that the unseen monsters of those dramas were more frightening than what horror films and TV portray so graphically today. Leiber engages the reader's imagination more completely, while avoiding the risk that movies run when viewers are aware of watching actors wearing monster suits or clockwork creatures crawling across Hollywood soundstages.

Conjure Wife was itself adapted twice for feature films. The first version was *Weird Woman* (1944), starring Lon Chaney, Jr., Anne Gwynne, and Evelyn Ankers. A higher-budget film was released under the title *Burn, Witch, Burn* (1962) starring Janet Blair, Peter Wyngarde, and Margaret Johnson. The screenplay, by science-fiction writer Richard Matheson and Charles Beaumont, was closer to Leiber's original novel version, although several incidents are altered. Tansy, for instance, holds out knowledge about witchcraft until the end and does not turn out to be the evil witch the audience has been led to suspect. *Burn, Witch, Burn* was released in England under the title *Night of the Eagle.*

Our Lady of Darkness was first published in 1977 and is perhaps Fritz Leiber's finest work, a culmination of his explorations into the conflict between the modern, rational mind and the unknown, unseen world beyond mankind's knowledge or control.

The novel represents an extension of the work in supernatural horror that began with his early short stories such as "Smoke Ghost" and in *Conjure Wife. Our Lady of Darkness* contains the best elements of the early works and a tribute to the many influences on his writings through the years. Once again we see his interest in tall buildings, the superstitious practices of modern people, and the horrors spawned by the urban environment.

Franz Westen is a forty-seven-year-old widower who has lived alone in San Francisco since his wife, Daisy, died of brain cancer four years earlier. He has been an alcoholic off-and-on most of his life and is just emerging from a long bout of heavy drinking that began when his wife died. He writes supernatural horror stories, lately earning his living from novelizations of a TV horror series. He adds authentic details to them, using a wealth of research material on science and pseudoscience. Sometimes he piles books and magazines on his bed in an informal arrangement he has come to think of as his "scholar's mistress," the substitute he has lately found for the companionship he once knew with his late wife.

His friends and neighbors in the old building include Gunnar (a computer scientist), Saul (a male nurse in a mental hospital), Fernando (a Latin-born janitor who does not speak English, with whom Franz plays chess), and Fernando's sister Dorothea Luque (who emigrated with him from Peru). Two floors below Franz lives a twenty-seven-year-old woman named Cal. The two have slept together twice and are friends, but Franz seems unsure of their relationship, partly because he is twenty years older than she.

Cal's full name is Calpurnia, the same as the Roman Cassandra who warned Caesar of danger several times. A Cassandra is a woman whose prophecies are ignored (from Priam and Hecuba's daughter Cassandra, fated by Apollo to deliver true prophecies but never to be believed). Cal, a professional musician who plays the harpsichord (among other instruments), first appears as she plays the recorder, her notes "dancing" upward to Franz's room through an empty airshaft. When Franz visits her afterward and mentions this, she replies, "Perhaps I did it to summon you. . . There's magic in music, you know." A reference is made to *The Magic Flute* and *The Enchanted Bassoon*, and he observes that music can levitate and fly up through the air. Also, Cal once visited the mental hospital where Saul works, and her recorder playing agitated the patients, while her piano music calmed them. She seems to be able to manipulate her listeners' emotions.

Franz and Cal's apartment building at 811 Geary plays a major role in the novel, which begins when he peers through binoculars across the city's rooftops from his seventh-story window. A one-thousand-foot-tall television tower (which at night constantly flashes lights) is in one direction, and in another, across a two-mile valley, lie the mountainous Corona Heights. A small park is located at its base. As he peers at the rocky protrusion, a skinny, tall human figure detaches itself from the background and apparently waves at Franz, moving its arms and dancing. Franz assumes the man must be a Haight-Ashbury mystic, "a stoned priest of a modern sun god dancing around an accidental high-set Stonehenge." Dismissing the sight as natural and normal, he picks up two books he has been reading and brings them down to Cal.

One is *Megapolistomancy: A New Science of Cities*, by a turn-of-the century author named Thibaut de Castries. This fictional *outré* thinker was frantic about the masses of steel, paper, kerosene, natural gas, and electricity being concentrated in major modern cities at the time. He opposed the building of the Eiffel Tower because he feared it might unleash forces of evil attracted by its mass of steel. Franz says this proved true, in a sense, as two world wars brought death and suffering to France. The de Castries "new science" of big cities encompassed fears of the ill effects of urban life on citizens. The most important menace was in the form of "paramentals," creatures formed by the evil elements found in cities.

The second book Franz shows Cal is one composed of blank rice-paper pages. A journal in violet ink fills one-quarter of the pages. He has reason to believe the journal author was Clark Ashton Smith, in real life a supernatural horror writer and follower of H. P. Lovecraft. Smith's handwritten notes were in black or blue ink, except for some sections in violet. This is one of the many points in the novel at which Leiber has blurred the lines between reality and fiction, placing the real Smith alongside the fictional de Castries.

The Smith journal in Leiber's novel mentions visiting de Castries at 607 Rhodes, and when Franz was shown the apartment number 607 he decided to take it, thinking it must have been some sort of predestined action. He speculates about the apartment building, with its disused broom closets, now sealed off, its airshafts, and even the capped vacuum system outlets, once used by the cleaning crews who attached hoses to vacuum the floors. Hidden rooms, walled-off areas that once served some purpose when the building was a hotel, and places that lie just beyond familiar walls all arouse Franz's curiosity.

He asks his friend Gunnar to bring home from his office a small paper-shredding device, so that he can describe the sounds it makes for a screenplay novelization. It makes "a faint, breathy buzzing, as if Time were clearing her throat." The tiny, shredded pieces of paper fall into a basket.

Later, Franz sees the creature in the distance again. This time, he hikes the two miles to Corona Heights to satisfy his curiosity. As Franz walks, he thinks about how de Castries would have hated today's buildings; the Bank of America Building and the Transamerica Pyramid make him remember a line of de Castries: "The ancient

Egyptians only buried people in their pyramids. We are living in ours." He called such buildings a "breeding ground for the worst of paramental entities."

Reaching Corona Heights, Franz looks back across the unfamiliar perspective of the rooftops near his own apartment building, knowing he will be able to spot his window since he saw this place through it earlier. He decides that "really, a city's roofs were a whole dark alien world of their own, unsuspected by the myriad dwellers below, and with their own inhabitants, no doubt their own ghosts and 'paramental entities.'"

A terrifying moment comes as he locates his window through binoculars and sees the slender figure waving at him, and by the time Franz arrives home, darkness has set in. He finds no intruder there, but a trail of paper shreds leads from the window to the bed.

Discussing all this with the nurse, Saul, and Cal, Franz wonders if he has been imagining things. He has battled alcoholism and has had very difficult periods of hospital cures, which included drugs. Cal tells him, "Why shouldn't a modern city have its special ghosts, like castles and graveyards and big old manor houses once had?" (This is the exact sentiment expressed in Leiber's short story "Smoke Ghost," in which a modern city had a sooty ghost composed partly of pollution.)

In bed later, Franz jokes with his scholar's mistress as a way of talking to himself. The pile now includes H. P. Lovecraft's *The Outsider,* yellowed copies of the old *Weird Tales* pulp magazines, some Clark Ashton Smith stories, and *The Collected Ghost Stories of Montague Rhodes James.* Then, reading in the de Castries book about cities, he finds a section in which the author concludes that "since we city-men already dwell in tombs, inured after a fashion to mortality, the possibility arises of the indefinite prolongation of this life-in-death. . . . without vitality or even thought, but only paramentation, our chief companions paramental entities of azoic origin more vicious than spiders or weasels."

Franz reads a journal entry where Smith discusses a visit to de Castries at "607" and is told of a "Fifty Book" and a "Grand Cipher." Smith is fearful. "Coming back today, I felt that my senses were metamorphosing. San Francisco was a meganecropolis vibrant with paramentals on the verge of vision and audition, each block a surreal cenotaph that would bury Dali, and I one of the living dead aware of everything with cold delight. But now I am afraid of this room's walls!" Smith also decries de Castries's gloating over the power that had caused the suicides of Jack London and fantasy poet George Sterling, and the disappearance of Ambrose Bierce; de Castries had decided they were "Judases" because they tried to leave his inner cult circle without his permission. Smith fears at this point that some terrible fate awaits him.

His interest spurred, Franz leafs through several books, one of which tells him that "civilization is being asphyxiated, mummy-wrapped by its own records, bureaucratic and otherwise, and by its infinitely recessive self-observations." He concludes that "truly, modern cities were the world's supreme mysteries, and skyscrapers their secular cathedrals."

Franz decides to go downtown to look up the history of his own building. The building permit was dated 1926 (fifty years earlier than 1976, the "present" of *Our Lady of Darkness*). This coincides with the "Fifty Book," if it means fifty years for something to take place. Franz takes home a city directory for 1927 to consult at his leisure.

Placing a bright piece of colored cardboard in his apartment window (to permit easier identification), he returns to Corona Heights. As he looks through his binoculars, the paramental entity (described as such for the first time) reaches out to Franz and somehow comes right through them. The entity is a "pale brown thing" with "a mask as narrow as a ferret's, a pale brown, utterly blank triangle, two points above that might mean eyes or ears, and one ending below in a tapered chin. . . . no, snout. . . no, very short trunk—*a questing mouth that looked as if it were for sucking marrow.*" Franz drops the binoculars and quickly leaves.

Rather than return home, he visits the painter Jaime Donaldus Byers, a man in his mid-forties who lives with bisexual young girls and studies the occult. Byers owns a rare copy of de Castries's book *Megapolistomancy*, too. He tells Franz that the writer finally turned against even his own works and tried to hunt down and burn every remaining copy, of which no more than a handful must now remain. He then turned against his former cult followers, resulting in his deadly vendettas against Jack London and Ambrose Bierce. A veiled woman companion was said to accompany de Castries on his travels, and a legend grew that she was an immortal "Queen of Night" and may have been from ancient Egypt.

As Franz handles the Smith book and gives it to Byers, Byers comes upon two pages that have been deliberately sealed together and finds a curse by de Castries against Smith:

> A curse upon Master Clark Ashton Smith and all his heirs, who thought to pick my brain and slip away, false fleeting agent of my old enemies. Upon him the Long Death, the paramental agony! when he strays as all men do. The fulcrum (0) and the Cipher (A) shall be here, at his *beloved* 607 Rhodes. I'll be at rest in my appointed spot (1) under the Bishop's Seat, the heaviest ashes that he ever felt. Then when the weights are on at Sutro Mount (4) and Monkey Clay (5) [(4) + (1) = (5)] BE *his Life squeezed away*. Committed to Cipher in my 50-Book (A). Go out, my little book (B) into the world, and lie in wait in stalls and lurk on shelves for the unwary purchaser. Go out, my little book, and break some necks!

The final phase of the novel takes place on the night of a symphony concert at which Cal is playing the harpsichord; Franz, Gunnar, and Saul are in the audience. Franz grows fretful and leaves the concert early, feeling that he must discover the secret of "607 Rhodes." At his apartment, he sets to work deciphering the curse. First, he hits on the meaning of "Monkey Clay"; it reminds him of "Monkey Wards," the nickname given to the Montgomery Wards department store by some people he had known who worked there.

Then, by placing a ruler along the intersection of Montgomery and Clay Streets, he plots a line to Mount Sutro and the TV tower, which also passes by Geary and Hyde (and his building). The current building at Montgomery and Clay is the Transamerica Pyramid. Franz concludes that Smith had been saved because the "weights" were not "on" (the building and TV tower had not been built) at the points mentioned in the curse until after Smith died.

Using the city directory for 1927, he looks through the 811 columns for a hotel on Geary Street, and it turns out to be the Rhodes. This means that "607 Rhodes" must have been his own apartment. He feels fearful again and wishes the concert were over and his friends would come home.

Placing more books and torn-out magazine stories on his bed, he contemplates how feminine the shape has become. The Lovecraft horror story "The Thing on the Doorstep" is lying on the open pages of a book; the Smith journal—open to the curse—and the de Castries book on cities are near the Clark Ashton Smith story, "The Disinterment of Venus." Various body parts, such as wide hips and a slender waist, seem to form his scholar's mistress.

In his depressed and fearful state, he decides that everything in his life is bad:

> And the entire world was just as bad; it was the perishing of pollution, drowning and suffocating in chemical and atomic poisons, detergents and insecticides, industrial effluvia, smog, the stench of sulphuric acid, the quantities of steel, cement aluminum ever bright, eternal plastics, omnipresent paper, gas and electron floods—electromephitic city-stuff indeed! though the world hardly needed the paranatural to do it to death. And the stars were even a swarm of phosphorescent fruit flies momentarily frozen in an utterly random pattern around a garbage planet.

Falling asleep on his bed, he has a terrifying nightmare. He dreams that his late wife Daisy is alive again, dying of cancer but having reached what he called the "vegetable stage," heavily drugged to relieve the pain. He realizes in the dream that his wife, who now grasps him with dry fingers, must really be dead. He tries to awaken, but the two rooms, his own and the room in his dream, have not fully merged with one another. He thinks he must have slept the night through but discovers that he only slept about one hour and is still alone.

Franz feels a hand on the back of his neck. It is his scholar's mistress, now animated as a paramental entity and starting to grasp his body with strong fingers, trying to smother him to death. He wrestles out of her grasp and falls to the floor, upsetting a coffee table and chess pieces.

He sees the creature in the moonlight:

> Then out of the darkness lifted there up, but not very high, the long, pale shape of his Scholar's Mistress. She seemed to look about her like a mongoose or weasel, her small head dipping this way and

> that on its slender neck; then with a nerve-racking dry rustling sound she came writhing and scuttling swiftly after him across the low table and all its scattered and disordered stuff, her long-fingered hands reaching out far ahead of her on their wiry long-pale arms.

Her hands grip him, and Franz screams as the creature again tries to suffocate him or crush him to death. He can see that

> her thin, wide-shouldered body was apparently formed solely of shredded and tightly compacted paper, mottled pale brown and yellowish with age, as if made up of the chewed pages of all the magazines and books that had formed her on the bed, while about and back from her shadowed face there streamed black hair. (The books' shredded black covers?). . . . [Her face was] narrow and tapering, shaped somewhat like a fox's or a weasel's, formed like the rest of her. . . It had no eyes, although it seemed to stare into his brain and heart. It had no nose. . . . The dry, rough, hard face pressed against his, blocking his mouth, squeezing his nostrils; the snout dug itself into his neck. He felt a crushing, incalculably great weight upon him. (The TV tower and the Transamerica! And the stars?) And filling his mouth and nose, the bone-dry, bitter dust of Thibaut de Castries.

Although we will not reveal the ending here, there is much more to be said about *Our Lady of Darkness.* Leiber added a number of autobiographical elements, blending these with fictional situations and characters. Asked about the apartment used in the novel, Leiber replied:

> I used the building where I was living at the time. Corona Heights viewed from my window suggested the idea of going out there and looking back at my window and imagining what would have happened if I had seen something. It involved me in looking up the history of the building, looking up when it was built and having to go down and do the things the hero did, at the assessor's office and so on.

The fictional de Castries was intended to present a view of modern cities.

> The de Castries character was just built up from whole cloth, and the idea there was just to have something that wasn't any traditional form of witchcraft, and I thought of someone who lived around 1890

> and thereabouts, or 1900, and would have seemed to be a natural precursor of the beatniks and hippies in a way, in the sense that he was a kind of back-to-nature person in some ways, and against big cities. Sort of having a lot of intuitive notions about big cities being bad. I'm ambivalent about big cities, myself. I'm quite a bit of a conservationist. However, the modern skyscraper is such an obvious expression of twentieth-century man. I mean, science-fiction authors find it difficult to be completely at war with something like that.

If the novel implied that cities were inherently bad and at the root of mankind's ills, then the ambiguity would not have been a problem, but Leiber doesn't set forth so simple an argument. Franz Westen finds much in cities to enjoy and at no time does he think of leaving for the country. The evil found in San Francisco resulted more from people like de Castries and his curse than from the masses of steel, electricity, or other substances in the urban environment.

It is significant that the humanist back-to-nature philosophy produces the deadly de Castries cult, which does not destroy the cities (as he planned) but ends up creating a mistrustful group of people who their own leader subsequently kills. The sorry end of the Manson cult and the tragic Jonestown episode are two examples of groups that broke away from confining, conventional life-styles. The de Castries group sought to conserve the natural environment in the face of pollution, the pillaging of natural resources, and the effects of industrial development. Leiber did not side with de Castries, although he did allow him to complain about the deterioration of the quality of urban life. In this way, he expressed his own ambivalence.

As Leiber said, however, no writer of science fiction can oppose totally the modern skyscraper and big cities; these represent technological achievement as well as symbolize the break with primitive living implicit in mankind's progress. Leiber did not select a wilderness setting to contrast with the evil cities (as Clifford D. Simak has done in *City* and other books). He allowed his own ambiguous attitude to be reflected in a villainous character who voiced some logical and intriguing arguments against cities, and a sympathetic character (Westen) who does not opt for a rural life-style regardless of his fears.

Leiber has written that he sometimes used his own fears as a starting point for story ideas. One case is his childhood fear of the dark:

> I had a dread of the dark that was a long time leaving me. . . . I wanted to be safe inside with my own people, my guardians, in my own lighted apartment. . . . I remember always taking an uneasy hour at least getting to sleep, especially during my apartment and school periods. I had occasional bad dreams and nightmares, though I wasn't steadily tormented with them as Lovecraft was. My worst ones came when I was trying to wake up and found myself in my familiar bed and room, with the creatures of my dreams still about me—clawed green hands reaching toward me out of secret panels and red-eyed skulls swooping about or peering at me from over the end of the bed. Now that I write these visions down, they seem to have a distinctly theatric, even melodramatic air. Did my dreams come from the stage? I'm not sure, though I do know *The Cat and the Canary* was responsible for some—it had secret panels. That was one trouble with safe apartments, incidentally—you never could be sure they didn't have secret panels, especially in the bedrooms behind the heads of the beds where they were hard to keep under observation.

These thoughts bear directly on *Our Lady of Darkness*. Much of the fearful activity takes place in the dark, and often in Franz's apartment. It was once safe and warm, when his wife Daisy was alive, but when she began to die, the place lost its pleasantness. Losing his wife meant a retreat into an isolated existence for Franz, and the type of childhood fears experienced by Leiber preyed upon him.

At the key moment of the book, Franz dreams that Daisy is alive again and sleeping with him. He tries to awaken but finds the room of his nightmare and the real-life one have merged. This was Leiber's childhood problem, compounded by imagined hands reaching out of panels and skulls staring at him over the end of his bed. Similarly the paramental suddenly spies Franz in bed, replacing his late wife's nightmare image with a fearful reality.

The idea of secret panels—another childhood fear—in the walls of an old apartment building derives from H. P. Lovecraft's type of horror (as does the idea of fearful paramental monsters who exist within modern cities). In the already-quoted Lovecraft passage about supernatural horror in literature, the writer noted that a "profound sense of dread" could be brought about by a story that included "a subtle attitude of awed listening, as if for the beating of black wings or the searching outside shapes and entities on the known universe's utmost rim." Leiber's novel includes these elements in a plausible contemporary setting. Franz's building contains something dreadful within the spaces just beyond its most mundane apartment walls and Franz has become the unwitting target of a curse that has brought a paramental entity to life.

Leiber differs from the Lovecraft approach in that his language and characterization are totally modern, in contrast with Lovecraft's typical use of stilted, archaic language, overblown prose, and minimal characterization. The Lovecraft protagonist was usually a loner who observed some sort of supernatural phenomenon, tracking it to its source. As with *Conjure Wife, Our Lady of Darkness* fits this profile (Norman Saylor as the alienated individualist on the trail of witchcraft, and Franz Westen as a sole investigator of the paramental he glimpsed at long range). However, Lovecraft's characters are misfits and neurotics with whom readers must strain to identify, while Leiber's average people are better-realized and more sympathetic.

As with *Conjure Wife,* Leiber chose to set *Our Lady of Darkness* in an ordinary place and populate it with ordinary characters. Unlike the robed sorcerers who live in fantasy's ancient castles and wave magic wands, Leiber's characters include an alcoholic widower and his neighbors in modern San Francisco—a nurse, a computer scientist, and a janitor. This helps make the book more terrifying, since we can relate to average people more easily than strange and exotic ones in distant locales. This approach to horror writing has been adopted by Charles L. Grant, Robert Bloch, Peter Straub, Stephen King, and other contemporary novelists.

We see music's role at the beginning and the end of *Our Lady of Darkness.* Cal's musical notes are said to dance and float up to Franz's room, and at the climax of the book, her playing of the fifth "Brandenburg Concerto" is important to the action. The magical properties of music were specifically mentioned and were also part of *Conjure Wife*; a Scriabin record had to be played as part of the ritual when Norman Saylor attempted to save Tansy's soul. Further, the mathematical element of music is related to the numerical and letter code made up by de Castries in his curse.

In the novel, Leiber interspersed many real and fictional names. This plays with our sense of history; we begin to wonder whether Jack London, Clark Ashton Smith, and others possibly did everything described in the novel. The interweaving of fact and fiction has lately become a popular technique of novelists, perhaps best exemplified by E. L. Doctorow's novel, *Ragtime*.

The name Daisy, for Franz Westen's late wife, is that of a flower. Fritz Leiber's wife was named Jonquil, another flower name, and she died after a long illness. *Our Lady of Darkness* was Leiber's first significant work of any major length following his lonely and depressed period after Jonquil passed away. Like the fictional Westen, he writes supernatural horror. Leiber, too, struggled with alcoholism for much of his adult life, including the time after Jonquil's death in 1969.

The origin of the novel's title occurs in a passage Franz comes across in a book. Although he does not realize he will soon confront a violent paramental who will embody the attributes of "Our Lady of Darkness," Franz learns in Thomas De Quincy's *Suspiria de Profundis,* that De Quincy described three "Ladies of Sorrow." The first is our Lady of Tears, who reminded Franz of the Virgin, as did the second, Our Lady of Sighs. The third sister, however, was Our Lady of Darkness, "defier of God," who is the "mother of lunacies and the suggestress of suicides." She "carries no key; for, though coming rarely amongst men, she storms all doors at which she is permitted to enter at all." Like the Three Furies of the classical world, these three sisters hold tremendous power.

There is no detailed explanation of how much of the third sister is found in the paramental, or of how de Castries's mysterious mistress fits into the transformation of the scholar's mistress. We learn that the dust of the cremated de Castries is somehow part of the paramental because Franz says this as the creature fills his mouth and nose with suffocating dust. The entity has two aspects of Our Lady of Darkness; she enters his room without a key, and she comes to him in the dark.

Women in this novel tend to be powerful and mysterious (as *many* have been in the works of Fritz Leiber). Even the paramental entity, the scholar's mistress, is given female attributes rather than male although at first it only existed as an inanimate pile of books and magazines. Cal, too, has a seemingly occult power in her musical performances, first at the mental hospital and later at the concert auditorium where her music spurs Franz to solve the mystery about "607 Rhodes." Her playing of the recorder in the early section of the book immediately precedes the first sighting of the paramental (who is "dancing," just as the recorder notes are).

A young woman at a bookstore causes Franz fear and guilt feelings because, during a drunken visit there, he has a vague notion that he had felt her body. Actually, she tried to playfully seduce him and is a precocious teenaged friend of Byers. And Franz is also afraid of testing his tentative relationship with Cal; he thinks he will make a fool of himself as a forty-seven-year-old pursuing a woman twenty years younger. Furthermore, Franz refers to a book called *The Spider Glyph in Time*, which contains musings about similarities between a woman's vagina and a spider waiting in a web—and a female entity, a "mistress," does menace him at the novel's end.

Daisy's power consists of her image in Franz's memory. He remembers his loving marriage in fond terms and yearns to have her back with him again. Her appearance in his nightmare has strong symbolic significance. The key to Franz's life has been his loneliness after she died, worsened by alcoholism and depression lasting for years and destroying his chances for a happy life.

He finds a substitute for Daisy in drinking, and then in the scholar's mistress. Lying in bed and reading, he drinks himself into a stupor to numb himself when he lets his mind wander into thoughts of Daisy's death. Now, rather than have his lifelong companion in bed with him, he has the safe and secure scholar's mistress there.

At the same time, however, he is contemplating a true relationship with Cal. So far, he has hesitated to explore what might develop, citing his age as an excuse. Viewed another way, Franz is afraid to get into a love affair because it would entail a lot of risk and effort, all of which could be avoided by staying solitary.

Daisy appears in the nightmare at the moment of crisis for Franz. He has tried to summon all of his courage, first to defeat alcoholism (and succeeding), and then to reach out to other people such as Cal and his other friends. Now he has pursued a frightening paramental vision he saw through binoculars. Rather than run away from this serious problem, he has been strong enough to confront it. Working mostly alone, he has tracked down the creature, unwittingly drawing it to his own bed.

The appearance of Daisy leads him to realize she is truly dead, as the dream graphically showed, describing her lifelike appearance turning into a terrifying skeletal apparition with vines growing quickly through her eye sockets and mouth. Perhaps his subconscious has for the first time admitted to the reality of her death, releasing Franz from his illusions. He need no longer cling to her memory so strongly that he can admit nothing else into his life. Now he can reach out to others.

Unfortunately, he reaches this crisis point just as the paramental entity takes over where the nightmare left off. Franz must now struggle for his life against the suffocating creature, who has replaced the alcoholism and loneliness that was, in a sense, suffocating him up to then. Franz is at a crossroads, and if he survives, he can go on to a new, more enriching life.

The loneliness Franz has endured is one aspect of the aging process for many people. No longer a young married man, Franz is approaching his fifties, in decline. His life would be enhanced by more activity, such as the recent socializing he has done, going to concerts with Gunnar and Saul. The drunken days and nights he describes took their toll on him by cutting him off from other people. In summoning his courage to defeat alcoholism, he has increased his contacts with his neighbors, playing chess, visiting them at home, and bringing them into his life by asking them for help in his quest to uncover the secrets of the paramental. In this way, *Our Lady of Darkness* is a novel about loneliness, courage, and self-discovery.

Chess plays a small role in this novel and is one of Leiber's interests. De Castries and Smith, replaced by Westen, play a sort of chess match. Franz has to move in prescribed ways, to certain prearranged points in order to avoid the curse, but then ends up in the worst place—in check by the curse. His movements to and from Corona Heights and his apartment resemble chess moves, especially because the lines of the Mount Sutro TV tower and the Transamerica Pyramid make up a grid of places where de Castries can exercise power.

As in the earlier novels such as *The Sinful Ones*, Leiber is describing the human predicament as being like a chess piece, with prescribed moves permitted. Urban man is given certain limits and can either go along with these or pay a price for rebelling. As in *The Sinful Ones*, Franz has chosen to struggle against the limits. Rather than leave the game (by moving to a new apartment building or perhaps simply avoiding the paramental by not chasing it), Franz has chosen to battle the problem head-on.

Leiber transforms everyday objects and average people into harbingers of horror. Franz imagines that a harmless parked car he passes on his way home from Corona Heights has tombstones instead of headrests. A normal apartment hallway seems fraught with danger. The windows on the Transamerica Pyramid look like the slots on computer cards. Other buildings take on fearful significance, as if waiting to become the tombs of unwary citizens.

Tall buildings have played a part of several Leiber writings, including "Smoke Ghost" (a story in which the urban environment spawns a ghost composed of sooty pollution and the hates and fears of the city dwellers), and "The Button Molder" (in which a future New York becomes a nightmare of skyscrapers inundated by waste products). In *Our Lady of Darkness*, skyscrapers appear menacing to Franz. He likens them to "tombs" for the unsuspecting victims of entities that seem to play hide-and-seek among the buildings. He quotes from de Castries about the unhealthy influence of the concentrations of steel in the structures of tall buildings and bridges.

Buildings are what monuments were to ancient civilizations. Someone like de Castries might call our structures mausoleums, but they could also be towering symbols of progress that rose out of the wilderness, representing the technological breakthroughs of the era (plumbing, heating, air conditioning, and electric lights, followed by computers, television, and satellite dish networks for communication). Backward or primitive societies, where disease and famine were once threats to life, have taken pride in their modern cities with skyscrapers. Cities such as Detroit, Atlanta, and Cleveland have centered their urban renewal efforts around skyscraper clusters, complete with shining towers, taller than the older buildings. A Detroit "Renaissance Center" was built to symbolize the city's attempts to recover from urban decay, and its towers now appear on most promotional literature for the city. Through the years, cities have competed to build the tallest skyscrapers in America. All this shows the significance attached to skyscrapers, seemingly little different than in primitive civilizations, where the tallest monument or pyramid symbolized supremacy of a people.

But as Leiber characterizes them in his fiction, they are objects of fear, and an interesting Freudian interpretation suggests itself. Much as a young boy might fear his father's penis, larger and more powerful than his own, so might a person fear a phallic building. *Our Lady of Darkness* specifically refers to this. As Saul describes the irrational fears of a mental patient, he says: "Mrs. Willis says the skyscrapers get very heavy at night when they—excuse me—screw her. . . Can't you imagine their tall gray skinny forms sneaking sideways down the streets, one flying buttress erected for a stony phallus?" While such metaphors are thought-provoking, one must remember that Leiber was writing a fictional work and may not have the irrational fears he describes in his novel. Rather, he has a love-hate relationship with buildings and huge cities and has always chosen to live in cities such as Chicago and San Francisco when given a choice.

But there might be significance to the purposeful use of the anima in *Our Lady of Darkness*. The psychologist Carl Jung called a female figure who represents the projection of a male's ideas of a woman an anima, while the animus represents male characteristics as perceived by the female mind. Jung theorized that the anima and animus represent the opposed archetypal characteristics of the two sexes, which people mask with sexual stereotypes and repress as part of their self-image. In fantasy or in a perceived reality altered by the man's mind, his unconscious projects this anima outward. According to theory, the relationship between a man and a woman can be disrupted by this projection, since it prevents a confrontation with the true personality of the other person as she exists.

Jungian archetypes are primeval images and symbols in the collective or racial unconscious. These appear in fairy tales, folk stories, myths, religious allegory, and fiction. The female creature in *Our Lady of Darkness* is obviously an anima of Franz Westen's mind. Westen's yearning for a companion to replace his lost wife, and the significant nightmare he had just prior to the animation of the scholar's mistress show that his mind was attuned to the creation of an anima.

Transformations take place in several Fafhrd and Gray Mouser stories, such as "Adept's Gambit," in which women are turned into sows as part of a curse, and people are turned into other people, ghosts turn into solid images, and statues turn into gods. The transformation of the paper and books into the scholar's mistress creature in this novel is the most dramatic in Leiber's works.

On a less dramatic scale, all writers of fiction take the materials found in their lives, including the influences of other writers' works and the overheard conversations of strangers, and use them in their writing. When Leiber chose to have Franz Westen's paramental entity be composed of Lovecraft, Smith, *Weird Tales,* and other works, he was paying tribute to their influence on his own writings, but also was, in a sense, showing what a writer's anima might form itself from as it took shape. In short, it seems clear that Leiber put a great deal of himself into *Our Lady of Darkness.* Perhaps as a result, he created one of his most powerful works.

7

Notable Short Fiction

Fritz Leiber has published over two hundred pieces of short fiction, including several award-winners. Space does not permit a discussion of more than a handful of his stories, but he has written successful parodies, satire, humor, Lovecraftian horror, modern horror, hard science fiction, and antiwar stories. Various subjects find their way into these, such as chess, cats, fencing, pacifism, and the previously mentioned concern with modern cities.

The award-winning story "Belsen Express" is about a modern man, George Simister, whose main interest is making money. He grumbles about Jews and Slavs when he reads his morning newspaper and argues with more compassionate people, such as his acquaintence Holstrom, with whom he rides the subway daily. Simister has developed a paranoid obsession about the Gestapo returning from World War II (now long past) to knock on his door, take him to a crowded motor van, and kill him and other prisoners with carbon monoxide fumes piped into the van. Although Simister lives in a world supposedly safe from World War II Europe, he fears "something reaching out across the dark Atlantic to threaten his life, his security, and his confidence that he would never have to suffer pain except in a hospital."

Leiber plants small fears in innocuous places, slowly building toward the climax. At the subway station, Simister gets shoved into a line of people who must part left or right, reminding him of the lines at German concentration camps, where one line went to immediate death and the other to hard labor. The destination on his subway car becomes "Belsen Express" instead of "Express," as if he were going to a concentration camp. Three books about Nazi war crimes arrive mysteriously at his home. Someone knocks loudly on his front door but disappears when he answers it. Although his friend has sent him the books to try to change his thinking, and neighborhood pranksters may have knocked on the door and run away, Simister has been unable to rid his mind of fear.

Finally, he dies in his office. The first doctor diagnoses carbon monoxide poisoning by the obvious symptoms, but a second one decides to rule the death is a case of heart failure.

"Belsen Express" is related to Leiber's stories such as "The Button Molder" and his novel *Our Lady of Darkness;* in all of these he says that modern man is not invulnerable to danger simply because he has mastered science or logic. Superstition or occult forces arrayed against a lone observer can be as perilous today as in primitive times. The insulation George Simister feels in "Belsen Express" is quickly eroded once the inexorable movement of evil starts in motion. Security and self-satisfaction are both destroyed by the fear in his mind.

"237 Talking Statues, Etc." is about a man much like Leiber himself, son of a great and aristocratic actor who had life-masks, statues, and portraits done of himself in his favorite acting roles, such as Macbeth. The son then hears his dead father speaking to him through the various effigies around him. Although tormented by the overshadowing image of his father's reputation and dominating personality, the younger man finally comes to understand his father. He sees that his father has begun to feel trapped by his very power and is weary of it. He is also tired of being forced to live on in the old acting roles, through the existence of the effigies. This story is written with full stage dialogue directions as if it were a play.

A television screenplay, *The Mechanical Bride,* was nearly produced for the series *Tales of Tomorrow* in the early 1950s and was later published in *The Second Book of Fritz Leiber* (1975). In it, a woman's effigy is turned into a working and lifelike robot, based on the theory that a man only wants a beautiful but brainless female as a companion. At the end of the screenplay, the man cannot tell whether he is with the real or artificial woman. The robot woman then kills him. The story was named after a 1951 Marshall McLuhan book of the same title. McLuhan had written about men who seem content with *Playboy* centerfold women or unintelligent actresses with attractive faces and figures, rather than real women who could converse with them and be looked upon as equals. Leiber's story places the sexist man in an unfavorable light.

"Gonna Roll the Bones" won the Hugo Award for best short story. Joe Slattermill gets into a dice game and gradually learns that he has been lured by the Devil into a gamble that will decide whether or not he will lose his soul for eternity. Many consider this to be one of Leiber's best stories. His use of background, gambling terms, and folk magic employed by the seemingly simple country women to protect their men create a colorful and exciting story.

In "Richmond, Late September, 1849," Leiber writes about Edgar Allan Poe's mysterious last days. In the story, Poe feels death approaching and senses the impending Civil War.

In the story "Waif," a twelve- or thirteen-year-old girl finds the losts cat of the narrator, who lives with his depressed, alcoholic wife. His own daughter died at the same age, and his wife and he have been unhappy ever since. He feels a mixture of sexual attraction and guilt as he talks with the girl. He consults Norman Saylor, from *Conjure Wife,* who lives across the street. Saylor advises the man that the girl might be the man's anima, his Jungian female archetype.

In this strange story, the girl tries to entice the man to leave with her, presumably to another planet near Orion. She then attempts to shoot the man's wife with a toy pistol, but he stops her. Prior to this, the man and his wife have had to defend his reputation from an unfair charge of child molestation involving the girl.

Two of Leiber's stories are of significance because they are related to *Our Lady of Darkness* and Leiber's concerns in that novel. One, "Black Glass," is written from the viewpoint of an unnamed narrator, possibly Leiber himself, or a fictional approximation of him. On vacation in New York City partly to visit his son, he feels oppressed by the changes he sees in the city since his visit twenty years earlier. Most buildings now have black glass in this metropolis, where "the violence seething just below the surface in the city was as real as the filth upon that surface, and skyscrapers had reason to foresee doom and robe themselves in black." He cites filth, pollution, noise, the near-bankruptcy of the city government, the retrenchment of the universities due to falling revenues, and the now-silent cab drivers who huddle behind their bullet-resistant enclosures and take payment through a slot as evidence that the skyscrapers were appropriately faced with black glass "as though they were glisteningly robing themselves for an urban funeral—perhaps their own."

As so often happens in Leiber's stories, the man begins to have difficulty distinguishing between mundane events and those with sinister implications. He fears that his eyes are giving him trouble—reminding him of his dread of going blind from retinal degeneration, recently cured through laser treatments—when he perceives a darkening of the city. This might have been because he was looking through black glass, but when he leaves the building he sees that the city is indeed darker.

He once encountered a young woman skating at Rockefeller Center with a man in a lion suit. He now sees her again and she mouths words to him in the distance, telling him, "Cortlandt Street. Tower Two. The Deck." He knows this means the Observation Deck of the southernmost tower of the World Trade Center and goes to meet her there.

On the subway, he meets an old Jewish man who talks incessantly of the "black foam" and the "dreck" that has begun to engulf New York. He claims this filthy substance has begun to accumulate on the streets and sidewalks and that it no longer washes off. People ignored it, he says, "pretended it wasn't there, like they always do at first with muggings and trashings and riots and war and death. But I could see it." According to his chemistry-student son, the dreck is a black, monomolecular, unbiodegradable, paraterminal waste product. The son told him it is formed by the catalytic action of wastes, "as if the organic, under unprecendented pressures, were trying to return to the inorganic, and succeeding only too well."

The narrator reaches the World Trade Center and feels a sudden urge to leap onto the elevator just before its doors close. He feels some sort of force field as he crosses the line to enter the elevator and then thinks he hears odd, animallike breathing in the empty car. The loudspeaker is silent, whereas the day before it had informed passengers they were moving at a quarter-of-a-mile in under one minute.

The narrator seems to have traveled in time, because he sees a group of robed figures silently readying large guns to fire at other tower dwellers. These people exist in a future New York, in which the black substance has totally covered the surface of the city. The man recalls a line from Macbeth, "Make the gruel thick and slab," from the cauldron scene. The black material has become a thick ocean that has left only the tallest buildings above it, and only the highest floors of those.

The young woman he saw earlier tells him he is from "Elsewhen" and that she trusts him to help her in her mission to stop the robed men from killing the other survivors in the distance. People have turned against one another rather than cooperate to fight the black foam. Cooperation is mankind's only hope, she says. She hands him a black lion statuette cube that matches hers and tells him it can give some oxygen if necessary. Later she leaps or falls from a crude bridge between towers during a raygun fight. The man concludes she must have survived in the foam ocean, thanks to the cube's oxygen.

Returning to the present, the man meets his son and then goes to a hospital for rest. Upon his release the next day, he decides he must have had a hallucination, except that he still carries the lion statuette and believes it is made of some unknown substance. He thinks he saw a future New York that will come true if the present trends continue.

We see in "Black Glass" the traditional view of time travel in science fiction: present trends can be altered to avert a future. This is a warning story, similar to H. G. Wells's and others, in that it threatens unhappy future consequences of present conditions.

"The Button Molder" is set in a modern city and told in the first person by an unidentified narrator, who sees a manikin in a store window. He gets the impression the faceless dummy is like the protohuman being into which the Button Molder threatens to melt down Peer Gynt. He muses that the lack of features allows the observer to fill them in, deciding whether the figure is male or female, pleasant or hostile.

He is a rooftop astronomer and also loves to peer at skyscrapers from overhead. He thinks it is essential to our mental health to reduce our tension and anxiety by gazing at the stars sometimes, so the conscious and unconscious halves of our minds can be balanced:

> I have the theory, you see, that in this age of mechanized hive-dwelling and of getting so much input from necessarily conformist artificial media such as TV and newspapers, its very important for a person to keep himself more directly oriented, in daily touch with the heavens or at least the sky, the yearly march of the sun across the stars, the changing daily revolution of the stars as the world turns, the crawl of the planets, the swift phases of the moon, things like that. After all, it's one of the great healing rhythms of nature like the seas and the winds, perhaps the greatest.

Leiber shares this theory, and his personal interest in rooftop astronomy (and gazing across city buildings from a height) has been reflected in this and other works. In *The Wanderer,* observers at widely separated points each thought the new planetoid was something different—a tiger's face, a yin/yang, or an angry god. Everyone had an intense interest in watching the heavens.

In "The Button Molder," the narrator is able to accept the idea of a weird apparition's appearance, partly because of his calmness gained through his previous sessions on the roof. In watching the night sky, he developed his ideas of the relationship between man and the changing views of heavenly bodies. Feeling closer to nature helps in confronting those things that science cannot easily explain.

On certain mornings, garbage trucks awaken the man, and he thinks of them as "sleep-shattering mechanical hogs." Leiber describes them in a poetic passage.

> It was an eerie and mysterious sight to see one of them draw up, say, at the big hotel across the street from me and an iron door in the sidewalk open upward without visible human agency and four great dully gleaming garbage cans slowly arise there as if from some dark hell. I found myself comparing them also (the trucks) to the Button Molder in *Peer Gynt.* Surely, I told myself, they each must have a special small compartment for discarded human souls that have failed to achieve significant individuality and were due to be melted down! Or perhaps they just mixed in the worn-out souls with all the other junk.

The narrator goes to the roof often and views the "secret world above the city." He thinks of the tall buildings as a guide and backdrop to his star-viewing, "exactly like with the menhirs at Stonehenge which primitive man used similarly." During one such session he observes three UFOs, shining objects he then finds are birds that caught light reflections. Another unidentified object, radiating a purple light, is observed traveling over distant buildings as if it were a chess piece moving over a chess board.

The man is a writer, fighting a severe writer's block. At one point he tries to write a page that would encompass his ideas about the world in succinct form. He thinks this led to the block. "If you could sum up all you felt about life and crystallize it in one master insight, you would have said it all and you'd be dead." The page shows he has an unresolved conflict over the definitions of fantasy and reality, and that he sees life as a struggle beginning at birth: to tell a single, simple story. He examines his writing and decides it is trash, suitable for being tossed into the maw of the big garbage trucks and taken away to be destroyed.

This state of mind leaves him ready for the appearance of a ghost. Slender, probably female, with glowing violet eyes (like the light he saw in the sky), she slips into his darkened apartment. Earlier, he imagined hearing and seeing a rustling figure, but this time it is apparent. He insists it is not simply the store manikin, although both lack features. This creature has a system of fine lines across its face and looks like "crazed or cracked pottery." It is taller than he, rather than small like the manikin.

Gripped by fright, he looks at the creature but dares not move; he fears certain death. He tries to make himself totally rigid, "like Roger Bacon's robot." The violet eyes stare into his and the single light bulb he turned on goes dead. The fine lines look like hair of some kind, and he hears a faint rustle as they seem to fall and sweep up as if to engulf him. Then the being fades back through the doorway.

He is now alone. He speculates:

> Was she perhaps an archetype of the unconscious mind somehow made real? the Anima or the Kore or the Hag who lays men out (if those be distinct archetypes)? Possibly, I guess. . . And what about

> the science fiction suggestiveness about her? that she was some sort of extraterrestrial being? That would fit with her linkage with a very peculiar violet star. . . Was she, *vide* Lang, a waking dream?—a nightmare, rather? Frankly, I find that hard to believe. Or was she really the Button Molder? (who in Ibsen's play, incidentally, is an old man with pot, ladle, and mold for melting down and casting lead buttons). That seems just my fancy, though I take it rather seriously.

Another possibility exists. Inside a part of the apartment's lowered ceiling near the entrance is a closed-off space. Reaching inside it, the man finds an old doll made of a material called Fabrikoid and stuffed with kapok: a 1920s doll made from an Oz character, in this case, the Patchwork Girl. "'What do you make of that?' I remember saying to myself, as I gazed down at it in my hand, somewhat bemused, '*Is this all fantasy ever amounts to? Scraps? Rag dolls?*'" The manikin is still in the store window, although he wonders if it was taken away by the garbage trucks.

We can see in "The Button Molder" the elements that went into several previous pieces of writing: a possible transformation, an anima, the autobiographical elements of a writer living alone in an apartment, and the slowly building feeling of terror from mundane surroundings. The man even wondered if the individuality of some people was strong enough to merit saving them from the button molder, thus tying the story in with Leiber's novels about individuality and nonconformity. As in *The Sinful Ones*, conscious effort at opposing the mass routine seems to enhance life. The man in "The Button Molder" considers the possibility that a strong enough personality might rescue a person from the oblivion of being enveloped by the button molder, just as being truly alive saved people in *The Sinful Ones*.

The steady variety of Leiber's short fiction is uncommon. Most SF or fantasy writers have made brief visits to the world of horror, humor, scientific extrapolation, sword-and-sorcery, or whatever else lies outside their usual sphere. But Lovecraft, Dunsany, and Clark Ashton Smith did not venture into hard SF, nor has King. Nor have Hal Clement and Ben Bova departed from their SF to do many fantasy stories. Most writers find a certain genre that suits their talents and interests and then base most of their short works on that foundation, while Leiber has been able to write dozens of tales in several different fields.

Leiber's longevity as a short-fiction writer has contributed to this. In science fiction, the usual practice is to write some short stories in the first two to five years as a professional, and then to switch to novels and series books. The effort required in short fiction surpasses by far that of a like number of pages within a novel; ten stories of twenty-five pages are harder to write than a novel of 250 pages. The new idea, background information, and brevity entailed in a short story demand more concise writing. Since SF poses the further problem of acquainting a reader with an alien world, new languages, and different social systems than exist on Earth today, a short story demands that a great deal of background information be presented in little space. Since the novel allows more room and a leisurely pace, most SF writers become novelists within a short time after their first story sales.

Leiber, on the other hand, has never abandoned short fiction. From his early career onward (including the 1980s) he has continued to add new stories to his works. For this reason, his collected short fiction fills several volumes and the copyright dates of their contents span five decades.

The writer's stories reflect many of the same concerns as his novels: individualism versus stifling conformity, the seemingly futile role of one person in an uncaring and vast cosmos (and the opportunities, nonetheless, for breaking through to great achievement), and that man's contemporary civilization has brought him no more security against the occult or the unknown than the primitive practices of his forebears.

8

Other Writings

Tarzan and the Valley of Gold is a Leiber novel outside the mainstream of his works. The creator of Tarzan, Edgar Rice Burroughs, is one of the most beloved figures in science fiction and fantasy. His Mars and Venus novels, as well as his Pellucidar books and Tarzan series, have endeared him to hundreds of millions of readers around the world in dozens of languages. The feature film *Tarzan and the Valley of Gold* was released in 1966, and Ballantine Books purchased the rights to a novelization of the Clair Huffaker screenplay; Leiber was chosen to write the book. Like those who write Sherlock Holmes stories, he had to please purists as well as the general audience. He also had to work within the confines of an existing screenplay. Somehow he managed to write a good book and to put something of himself into it.

The story concerns Tarzan and his attempt to stop a band of criminals, led by Augustus Vinaro, from capturing millions of dollars' worth of treasure left behind by the Incas in Tucumai, Peru. Before defeating Vinaro, Tarzan has to deal with Mr. Train, the man's massive bodyguard (who ends up being pushed into a well) and even some assorted thugs who ambush Tarzan in a car wash. A jungle boy named Ramel is kidnapped by the criminals when they learn that he knows the location of the lost city. Tarzan frees him.

The rather simple plot is the framework for the film and novel, where action must take precedence. One scene begins with Tarzan in the role of a bullfighter entering the bullring. The Mexican crowd is shocked to see that Tarzan has no toreador clothing and carries no implements to taunt or kill the bull. Using a rope and moving around the bull, he faces it and then manages to tame it, finally riding it, much as the ancient bull riders in Crete did. Following that taming incident, he insists that the promoters spare the animal and two other bulls as well and put them out to pasture as studs.

Leiber's pacifist leanings are well established. In *Tarzan and the Valley of Gold* he expressed his concern about war. The spectacle of a bloodthirsty crowd at a bullfight was abhorrent to a peaceful man, and Leiber described the bloody slaughter of another bull in terms that emphasized the sadism and cruelty of the act. In doing so, he added a reference to the wholesale murder a nuclear war could bring. "And all this in a world now threatened by an atomic death that might poison even the jungles and the seas, as well as wipe out mankind, a world that could no longer afford to nourish any cruelty or the least callousness toward the prospect of mass death."

Since this passage was not necessary to the plot it must be assumed that Leiber chose to insert it because he felt it belonged there. To a pacifist, death is upsetting even on a small scale, not just the obliteration of entire nations. If man wants to end war, he must confront the issue of individual violence as well as international conflict.

Leiber's references to the whites' treatment of South American Indians, even worse than their treatment of the Indians of this country, have a similar effect. The plot could have proceeded without such references, but Leiber's decision to add them showed his concern over this sorry aspect of the history of that region. Leiber sided with minorities in such works as *A Specter Is Haunting Texas,* and he apparently did not want to write about South America without mentioning the subjugation and exploitation of the Indians.

Tarzan and the Valley of Gold became number twenty-five in the popular Ballantine uniform edition of Tarzan books. Leiber's novel is the only one not written by Burroughs.

Leiber has also written poetry at various times during his career. While it has never taken center-stage, he has enjoyed writing it and has had the satisfaction of having it published from time to time in small press chapbooks.

In an interview about his poetry in *The Anthology of Speculative Poetry* in 1980, Leiber recalled that he had sometimes submitted his poems to SF magazines, but these rarely published poetry and his own seldom saw print. One was published in the special Fritz Leiber Issue of *The Magazine of Fantasy and Science Fiction* in July, 1969. *The Anthology of Speculative Poetry* reprinted several of his poems, including some that appeared in his novel *The Wanderer* and in the Fafhrd and Gray Mouser books.

To date, two collections of his poems have been published. *Demons of the Upper Air* is a chapbook edition published by Roy A. Squires (the SF and fantasy collector and publisher) in May, 1969. The hand-set poetry book was published in a limited edition of 275 signed copies and consists of twelve pages. Its contents deal with speculations about the types of "things" that could dwell on a roof above a city, coming down from the thin upper atmosphere where they usually live. Ghosts, nightmares, "the Elder gods," and batwings are alluded to in this evocative work. The demons are described as "ghosts. . . but with skeletons of steel" who "fly, black-winged, above." "The windswept, icy mountaintops of mind show tracks of our sharp claws."

The description of the demons contrasts them with the "Elder Gods," the deities of ancient times whose power is only revived today by arcane ritual. The Elder Gods are a convention in horror fiction, notably in Lovecraft's stories. Since the work was written in 1936, it is probable that Lovecraft's influence was strong as Leiber wrote *The Demons of the Upper Air*. The coexistence of ancient terrors with modern civilization is the primary thrust of the poem. Its formal, serious tone and language may be contrasted with the simple, straightforward prose that constitutes the major body of Leiber's work. Terms such as "squadrons," "eyrie," and "tramper on the road below" illustrate this.

In 1978, Squires published another poetry book in a limited edition of 265 copies on fine paper. Titled *Sonnets to Jonquil and All*, it consists of eight poems by Leiber and six poems by his late wife, Jonquil Stephens. This beautifully produced book also includes an afterword by Leiber detailing the background of the poems. This afforded him the opportunity to write about his beloved wife. He mentioned that Jonquil had been born in England on July 1, 1908 and that her paternal grandfather, Adrian Stephens, had invented the steam whistle in 1835, while her paternal grandmother, Emily

Stephens, had been a poet of note. Jonquil had attended Oxford University and the University of Chicago. She died on September 2, 1969 and is buried at Woodlawn Cemetery in Santa Monica.

Sonnets to Jonquil and All includes two about the Gray Mouser, the second of which begins:

> Soft-sandaled feet press lightly on the stones
> the cobble Lankhmar's mazy alleyways;
> A grayish cloak melts in the river mist. . .

The poem called "Santa Monica Beach at Sunset" refers to "the blast of bombs across the sea" and the "spectral" mood of the beach, where war can somehow reach across the ocean to strike fear in the narrator's heart. A sequel is titled "1959: The Beach at Santa Monica." Obviously written after World War II, it refers to knowing too much and feeling too much. It ends:

> Brace yourself against your atoms.
> The world is firm.
> The universe is sure.
> Return again to this knowledge.

Other writings by Leiber include his nonfiction work. Although he once considered writing a history of fantasy, he did not complete the research for the project. He has written hundreds of short pieces for a variety of publications, however, among them articles published by the encyclopedia companies that employed him after his graduation from the University of Chicago. Between 1945 and 1957, he wrote hundreds of articles and filler items for the magazine *Science Digest*. These ranged from astronomical articles to one about the tides that came out of the background information he compiled for *The Wanderer*. He served as assistant editor, and later, associate editor, for *Science Digest*, earning his principal income there before leaving to become a self-supporting, full-time freelance writer in 1957.

Leiber has written literary criticism on H. P. Lovecraft, notably the two essays that have been reprinted in several publications, including S. T. Joshi's book *H. P. Lovecraft: Four Decades of Criti-*

cism (1981). These essays are titled "A Literary Copernicus" and "Through Hyperspace With Brown Jenkin: Lovecraft's Contribution to Speculative Fiction." He also reviewed Lovecraft's *The Whisperer in the Darkness* in a review reprinted in *The Book of Fritz Leiber.*

Leiber has published many book reviews. He was the regular book review columnist for *Fantastic Stories,* beginning in March, 1968 and continuing through the magazine's change of format in March, 1979. He began contributing a regular column, "On Fantasy Books," to *Locus* magazine at that time. He also wrote a book review column in issues of *Fantasy Newsletter,* alternating his columns with those of Karl Edward Wagner on a bimonthly basis. Leiber dealt with fantasy fiction in an in-depth manner, often focusing upon the works Stephen King and other popular writers, having already established his reputation as one of the most knowledgeable reviewers in the genre.

Two paperback collections, *The Book of Fritz Leiber* and *The Second Book of Fritz Leiber* (1974 and 1975), contain a potpourri of fiction and nonfiction. Science articles, film criticism, essays on fantasy, and background pieces about his own writings make up the two collections.

Fritz Leiber's theater-trained speaking voice can be heard on two recordings for sale to the public. Alternate World Recordings offers a record album of the author reading a Fafhrd and Gray Mouser tale on one side, and the story "Gonna Roll the Bones" on the other. The record is titled *Fritz Leiber Reads "Gonna Roll the Bones".*

Hourglass Productions, a company that offers interviews with a select group of SF writers, sells a cassette tape about him. *An Hour with Fritz Leiber* contains an interview by writer Randall Garrett, in which Leiber details the origins of many of his major works and discusses his ideas about writing.

9

Fantasy, Reality, and the Unknown

Reflecting upon the body of work created by Fritz Leiber during his career, one finds certain themes and concerns that recur. Asked in 1982 to look back over his writings and summarize what he has been saying, Leiber said:

> I would say that all of my writing has increased my interest in the problem of the relationship between fantasy and reality. I believe I have discovered that the element of fantasy in storymaking is intimately and inextricably interwoven into the texture of reality. I tend less and less to think of separate worlds of reality and fantasy, but see them as interweaving, constantly, at all points. Whatever interpretation, whatever statement is made about reality has an element of fantasy, or story, in it, and vice versa.

This statement comes as no surprise to his readers. From the early stories onward, Leiber's characters have been rather ordinary people who found themselves in unusual or harrowing circumstances. In many of their adventures, Fafhrd and the Gray Mouser have confronted illusions and spells placed in their paths by demons and sorcerers. The first of their published exploits, "Adept's Gambit," features a singularly unpleasant curse that causes any woman they kiss to be transformed into a sow. In a story written decades later, "Under the Thumbs of the Gods," the pair are thwarted in every attempt to seduce women they encounter, but the reason this time is that the women are seeking revenge for all the times Fafhrd and the Gray Mouser have been sexually exploitive. The reality of the women's movement seems to have made an impression on Leiber, and he later said that he supports women's rights and wanted to bring this topic into a sword-and-sorcery tale involving his two heroes.

Reality and fantasy interweave in many of Leiber's stories and novels. The autobiographical elements in *Our Lady of Darkness* were discussed earlier, including the fact that his own apartment building and rooftop astronomy were its starting points. In this first major work after his wife's death, Leiber wrote of a novelist who was just coming out of a long period of mourning and whose battle against alcoholism reached a crisis point. Just as Franz Westen reached out to people to end his isolation, so did Fritz Leiber reach out by writing an important novel.

Franz Westen grappled with a paramental entity that assumes the place once occupied by his late wife, Daisy. That the entity took advantage of Franz's weakness and entered the scholar's mistress just as his nightmare was reaching its peak is an example of the battle Franz fought against delusion and fear. He questioned his own perception of reality throughout the novel, wondering if his eyes were playing tricks when he looked at the creature through his binoculars, and pondering whether he was being paranoid. The everyday objects in his environment (the car headrests he thought looked like small tombstones and the tall buildings that seemed to house hundreds of potential corpses in ready-made mausoleums) began to take on fearful significance to him. At the end of the book, Franz and the reader are not really sure where fantasy begins and reality ends.

Norman and Tansy Saylor in *Conjure Wife* are in a similar predicament. Is the faculty wife party the scene of a witches' plot or simply a place for campus politics and jockeying for tenure? Is the evil glance of one particular woman a sign that she intends a curse against Tansy? The same actions viewed from another perspective would indicate that only mundane purposes underly them, but a wealth of data has been growing to suggest the practice of witchcraft.

Norman is much less likely than Tansy to accept anything irrational or illogical, but his carefully wrought philosophy is torn apart when evidence of working magic is forcefully brought to his attention. The stone gargoyle that moves to his front porch and nearly gets inside to kill him and Tansy, a gargoyle pictured in photos he has seen in a woman's hands earlier, could have been brought there by fraternity members as a prank. Witchcraft is a more likely explanation, however, and even Norman is able to see that, despite the fact that he hates to admit anything unscientific. The battle against witches is paralleled by the battle inside his brain, where the rational and the antirational are fighting for control.

Individuality is another of Leiber's concerns. Fafhrd and the Gray Mouser strike out for freedom and adventure and hire themselves out to whatever patron has the money to send them on a mercenary assignment. While women seem to conspire to take the heroes' freedom away, the men strive to break out again. Scully maintains freedom of thought and action regardless of his shortcomings in *A Specter Is Haunting Texas,* and he leads a revolution to gain liberty for others. In *Gather, Darkness!* and *The Green Millennium,* repressive governments are in control, while rebellious Leiber heroes fight to overthrow them. The Wild Ones in *The Wanderer* are rebels, too.

The metaphor of mankind being like pawns in a vast cosmic chess match also appears in some of Leiber's writings. The Change War characters feel manipulated by unseen and enigmatic bosses whose nature might be good or evil, while the Earth in *The Wanderer* just happens to be in the way of a cops-and-robbers hot pursuit between space police and Tigerishka's Wild Ones. Franz Westen in *Our Lady of Darkness* moves across a chessboardlike grid laid over the city of San Francisco by the mystic de Castries, and he tries to avoid being placed in check by staying away from the lair of the paramental entity.

The theme of pacifism is found in stories such as "Richmond, Late September, 1849" and the collection *Night of the Wolf*. Satire is used effectively in *The Green Millennium, The Silver Eggheads,* and *A Specter Is Haunting Texas*. Each also includes a rebellious Leiber hero and makes a statement in favor of the individual in society. The writers who try to do their own work when replaced by machines in *The Silver Eggheads,* and Phil Gish, who opposes the Department of Morality and the Bureau of Loyalty in *The Green Millennium,* are people whose lives have been controlled by others and who decide to fight back.

City skylines and the tall buildings that compose them have appeared in "The Button Molder," "Smoke Ghost," *Our Lady of Darkness*, and other Leiber works. His personal interest in rooftop astronomy and gazing across cities from heights led him to write "Black Glass," among other tales. Buildings have taken on good and bad qualities in his fiction, including the menace to Franz Westen and the peaceful serenity and healing influence afforded to the narrator of "The Button Molder." This reflects Leiber's feelings of ambivalence in his love-hate relationship toward big cities.

Women and their relationships with men are important in most Leiber works. The Fafhrd and Gray Mouser stories feature a particularly possessive and vindictive mother, whose Snow Women cohorts would rather have their men die than set free. Most of the other women in Leiber fiction appear in a more favorable light, and their relationships with men are vital to the outcome of the stories. Together, men and women mount a good battle against the forces they confront, but apart, they founder.

Norman disbelieves Tansy's theories about magic; this results in deadly danger to both people. Cal helps the lonely widower Franz Westen get over the loss of his wife Daisy, and this becomes crucial in his fight against the female paramental entity. Alone, however, he is in peril. The two main characters in *The Sinful Ones*, Carr and Jane, are in a similar situation. They may be the only people truly alive, except for the evil group of conspirators hunting for them, and each was in worse trouble alone than as a couple. Tigerishka and Paul in *The Wanderer* do not get along at first, but their mating ends up influencing Tigerishka to heal the Earth's wounds and spare its people from greater losses. Before her relationship with Paul, she was totally uncaring about humans and disdainful of them. At one point, too, the Wanderer appears as a yin/yang symbol—representing the male and female principles of the universe in Chinese cosmology—while at another moment, observers on Earth call it an angry animal face. These images signify the joining of alien and man as Tigerishka and Don make love, the joining and cooperation of male and female which begins the healing process.

Asked what he has derived from a life devoted in large part to science fiction and fantasy, Leiber said, "Well, I've gotten a way of life out of it. And a way of looking at myself and life that is forever involved with writing." He intends to go on writing as long as he can, with no plans to retire. What has kept him interested in these genres rather than others where he might have practices his craft? Leiber replied:

> I think that it's the pursuit of the unusual and the unknown. I somehow feel that a story is incomplete without that element. So it's my pursuit of the strange, the unusual, and my concern with the interface between the unknown and the known. That always seems to me to be an important part of a story, and so the stories I write continue to fall into the fantasy, science fiction, or supernatural horror fields.

In his seventies, Fritz Leiber keeps on writing stories that delight his audience, readers who have come to expect great writing from this grand master of the imagination.

Notes

PAGE	QUOTE	SOURCE

1. Master of All Trades

PAGE	QUOTE	SOURCE
2	"just sound in its way"	Author's interview with Fritz Leiber, 1981.

2. The Biting Edge: Satire

PAGE	QUOTE	SOURCE
5	"an easier night's writing"	Fritz Leiber, *The Silver Eggheads* (New York: Ballantine, 1979), p. 7.
5	"licensed to wear Levis"	Ibid., p. 8.
6	"Gaspard de la Nuit"	Ibid., pp. 12–13.
6	"the near-hypnotic wordmill product"	Ibid., p. 12.
6	"He wrote his latest bestseller"	Ibid., p. 13.
7	"Homer Hemingway axed through"	Ibid., pp. 19–20.
8	"a kind of alcoholic parlor football"	Ibid., p. 30.
8	"Naturally a machine"	Ibid., p. 30.
12	"signs saying 'restricted'"	Fritz Leiber, *The Green Millennium* (Boston: Gregg Press, G. K. Hall, 1980), p. 12.
13	"Not that this current social madness"	Ibid., p. 43.

PAGE	QUOTE	SOURCE
13	"She was not an ordinary girl"	Ibid., p. 47.
14	"Psychologists, he supposed"	Ibid., p. 53.
15	"housing shortage alluded to"	Ibid., p. 14.
16	"platform shoes worn"	Ibid., p. 196
16	"specially-bred green cats"	Ibid., p. 204.
17	"Ever since Lyndon ousted Jack"	Fritz Leiber, *A Specter Is Haunting Texas* (New York: Daw Books, 1978), p. 5.
18	"Dallas, Texas, Texas"	Ibid., p. 10.
18	"Scully, son, ever since"	Ibid., p. 10.
19	"You see, Scully"	Ibid., p. 17.
20	"because of the grandeur"	Ibid., p. 28.
20	"Ronald the Third"	Ibid., p. 31.
21	"It had been an ideal country"	Ibid., pp. 140–41.

3. Freedom, Nonconformity, and Alienation

PAGE	QUOTE	SOURCE
25	"I was fascinated by the idea"	Fritz Leiber, *The Sinful Ones* (Boston: Gregg Press, G. K. Hall, 1980), p. 172.
26	"When Carr Mackay first caught sight"	Ibid., p. 5.
26	"it was as if Carr"	Ibid., p. 7.
26	"Right there Carr got the feeling"	Ibid., p. 7.
26	"Don't you really know"	Ibid., p. 11.
27	"What if the whole world"	Ibid., p. 16.
27	"Wasn't there a sense"	Ibid., pp. 19–20.
28	"There he was"	Ibid., p. 21.
28	"blundered into one of those"	Ibid., p. 26.
30	"You're born with a feeling"	Ibid., p. 147.
30	"I wonder if we haven't been wrong"	Ibid., pp. 169–70.

PAGE	QUOTE	SOURCE
32	"Some stories of terror"	Fritz Leiber, *The Wanderer* (Boston: Gregg Press, G. K. Hall, 1980), p. 9.
32	"So we might begin this story"	Ibid., pp. 10–11.
34	"If beings were that advanced"	Ibid., p. 106.
37	"But what must we understand"	Ibid., p. 309.
38	"I thought, if the scientists"	Jim Purviance interviews Fritz Leiber, *Algol* (Summer/Fall, 1978), p. 25.
42	"from everyone and to each"	Fritz Leiber, *Gather, Darkness!* (Boston: Gregg Press, G. K. Hall, 1980), p. 96.
44	"trying to dream of an insanity"	Fritz Leiber, *Night of the Wolf* (Aylesbury, England: Sphere Books, 1976), p. 25.
44	"The newly purchased tickler"	Ibid., p. 37.
47	"before the big propaganda engines"	Ibid., p. 178.
47	"as if there were a silent wolf-pack"	Ibid., p. 172.
47	"you are not asked to kill"	Ibid., p. 192.

4. Try and Change the Past

PAGE	QUOTE	SOURCE
50	"Change one event in the past"	Fritz Leiber, *The Change War* (Boston: Gregg Press, G. K. Hall, 1978), p. 81.
50	"we can hardly expect"	Fritz Leiber, *The Big Time* (Boston: Gregg Press, G. K. Hall, 1976), p. 62.
51	"My job is to nurse back"	Ibid., p. 5.
51	"You don't know about the Change War"	Ibid., pp. 5–6.
53	"The Place is a regular theater"	Ibid., p. 17.
56	"If you wanted to time-travel"	Ibid., p. 29.

PAGE	QUOTE	SOURCE
58	"Most men are simply not equipped"	Ibid., p. 147.
60	"My masterpiece"	Fritz Leiber, *Destiny Times Three* (New York: Dell Publishing, 1978), p. 250.
60	"A drastic simplification"	Ibid., pp. 250–51.
61	"tree of life"	Ibid., p. 10.
61	"like a devil-may-care Satan"	Ibid., p. 12.
64	"We will watch your future"	Ibid., p. 146.
65	"He wondered what was happening"	Ibid., p. 132.

5. Sword-and-Sorcery: Fafhrd and the Gray Mouser

PAGE	QUOTE	SOURCE
67	"Fafhrd and Mouser are rogues"	Fritz Leiber, *Swords of Lankhmar* (Boston: Gregg Press, G. K. Hall, 1977), p. 5.
68	"For all do fear the one"	Fritz Leiber, *Night's Black Agents* (Boston: Gregg Press, G. K. Hall, 1980), Foreword.
68	"His light chestnut hair"	Ibid.
69	"it is perfectly clear that Leiber"	Ursula K. Le Guin, *The Language of the Night* (New York: Berkley/Putnam, 1979), pp. 91–92.
70	"Each Snow Woman, usually with the aid"	Fritz Leiber, *Swords and Deviltry* (Boston: Gregg Press, G. K. Hall, 1977), p. 16.
70	"believes that both pleasure and rest"	Ibid., p. 39.
70	"Vlana ought to be whipped"	Ibid., pp. 49–50.
71	"Women are horrible"	Ibid., p. 115.
71	"Travel, love, adventure"	Ibid., p. 119.
71	"There is a witchy cold"	Ibid., p. 116.

6. Creatures of Darkness: Horror

PAGE	QUOTE	SOURCE
74	"That spring we'd driven out"	Fritz Leiber and Stuart Schiff, eds., *The World Fantasy Awards, Volume 2* (Gar-

PAGE	QUOTE	SOURCE
		den City, New York: Doubleday, 1980), p. xiii.
75	"The one test of the really weird"	H. P. Lovecraft, *Supernatural Horror in Literature* (New York: Dover, 1973), p. 16.
76	"In my view of the universe"	August Derleth and James Turner, eds., *H. P. Lovecraft: Selected Letters, 1934–1937,* vol. 5 (Sauk City, Wisconsin: Arkham House, 1976), pp. 356–57.
77	"narrow unamiable culture with its taboos"	Fritz Leiber, *Conjure Wife* (Boston: Gregg Press, G. K. Hall, 1977), pp. 6–7.
78	"a young warrior and squaw who"	Ibid., p. 8.
84	"Actually, it was based partly"	Author's interview with Fritz Leiber, 1981.
86	"Perhaps I did it to summon you"	Fritz Leiber, *Our Lady of Darkness* (New York: Berkley/Putnam, 1978), p. 10.
86	"A stoned priest of a modern sun god"	Ibid., p. 7.
87	"a faint, breathy buzzing"	Leiber, *Our Lady of Darkness,* p. 20.
87	"The ancient Egyptians only buried"	Ibid., p. 21.
88	"breeding ground for the worst"	Ibid., p. 27.
88	"Really, a city's roofs"	Ibid., p. 29.
88	"Why shouldn't a modern city"	Ibid., p. 37.
88	"Since we city-men already dwell"	Ibid., p. 64.
88	"Coming back today, I felt"	Ibid., p. 66.
89	"civilization is being asphyxiated"	Ibid., p. 69.
89	"truly, modern cities were"	Ibid., p. 70.
89	"a mask as narrow as"	Ibid., p. 84.
90	"A curse upon Master"	Ibid., pp. 121–22.
91	"And the entire world was just as bad"	Ibid., p. 168.
91	"Then out of the darkness"	Ibid., p. 173.
92	"her thin, wide-shouldered"	Ibid., pp. 174–75.

PAGE	QUOTE	SOURCE
92	"I used the building where I was living"	Author's interview with Fritz Leiber, 1981.
92	"the de Castries character was just"	Ibid.
94	"I had a dread of the dark that was"	Leiber and Schiff, pp. xx–xxi.
96	"carries no key; for, though coming rarely"	Leiber, *Our Lady of Darkness*, p. v.
97	"Franz refers to a book"	Ibid., p. 165.
100	"Mrs. Willis says the skyscrapers"	Ibid., pp. 38–39.
100	"But there might be significance"	For a brief discussion of anima in lay terms, see H. J. Eysenck and W. Arnold, *Encyclopedia of Psychology*, vol. 1 (New York: Herder and Herder, 1972), pp. 55, 78–79.

7. Notable Short Fiction

PAGE	QUOTE	SOURCE
102	"something reaching out across the dark"	Fritz Leiber, *Heroes and Horrors*, Stuart David Schiff, ed. (New York: Pocket Books, 1980), p. 104.
104	"the violence seething just below"	Ibid., p. 57.
105	"as though they were glisteningly robing"	Ibid., p. 56.
105	"pretended it wasn't there"	Ibid., p. 68.
105	"as if the organic"	Ibid., p. 69.
107	"I have the theory, you see"	Stuart David Schiff, ed., *Whispers III* (Garden City, New York: Doubleday, 1981), p. 150.
107	"It was an eerie and mysterious"	Ibid., p. 155.
108	"exactly like with the menhirs"	Ibid., p. 154.
108	"If you could sum up all you felt"	Ibid., p. 175.
108	"was she perhaps an archetype"	Ibid., pp. 176–77.

PAGE	QUOTE	SOURCE
109	"What do you make of that?"	Ibid., p. 177.

8. Other Writings

PAGE	QUOTE	SOURCE
112	"And all this in a world now"	Fritz Leiber, *Tarzan and the Valley of Gold* (New York: Ballantine, 1966), p. 21.
112	"In an interview about his poetry"	Robert Frazier, ed., "Fritz Leiber Interview," *The Anthology of Speculative Poetry* 4, 1980, pp. 24–25.
113	"ghosts. . . but with skeletons of steel"	These and all other quotations from *The Demon of the Upper Air* are from unnumbered pages of *The Demons of the Upper Air* (Glendale, California: Roy A. Squires, 1969).
114	"Soft-sandaled feet press lightly on"	Fritz Leiber, *Sonnets to Jonquil and All* (Glendale, California: Roy A. Squires, 1978), p. 8.
114	"blast of bombs across the sea"	Ibid., p. 9.
114	"Brace yourself against your atoms"	Ibid., p. 9.

9. Fantasy, Reality and the Unknown

PAGE	QUOTE	SOURCE
116	"I would say that all of my writing"	Author's interview with Fritz Leiber, 1982.
119	"Well, I've gotten a way of life"	Ibid.
120	"I think that it's the pursuit of the unusual"	Ibid.

Bibliography

Works by Fritz Leiber

Novels

Gather, Darkness!. New York: Pellegrini and Cudahy, 1950.
Conjure Wife. New York: Twayne, 1953. Later published as *Burn, Witch, Burn*. New York: Berkley, 1962.
The Green Millennium. New York: Abelard, 1953.
The Sinful Ones. New York: Universal, 1953. Revised edition. New York: Pocket Books, 1980. Shorter version published as *You're All Alone*. New York: Ace Books, 1972.
Two Sought Adventure. New York: Gnome Press, 1957.
Destiny Times Three. New York: Galaxy, 1957.
The Big Time. New York: Ace Books, 1961.
The Silver Eggheads. New York: Ballantine, 1962.
The Wanderer. New York: Ballantine, 1964.
Tarzan and the Valley of Gold. New York: Ballantine, 1966.
The Swords of Lankhmar. New York: Ace Books, 1968.
Swords against Wizardry. New York: Ace Books, 1968.
A Specter Is Haunting Texas. New York: Walker, 1969.
Swords and Deviltry. New York: Ace Books, 1970.
Swords against Death. New York: Ace Books, 1970.
Swords and Ice Magic. New York: Ace Books, 1977.
Rime Isle. Chapel Hill, North Carolina: Whispers Press, 1977.
Our Lady of Darkness. New York: Berkley/Putnam, 1977.
Bazaar of the Bizarre. West Kingston, Rhode Island: Donald M. Grant, 1978.

For purposes of this listing, all volumes containing only stories of Fafhrd and the Gray Mouser are here listed as novels, although only *The Swords of*

Lankhmar is a full-length novel. Books that contain related stories in that series and are listed here rather than as collections include *Two Sought Adventure, Swords against Wizardry, Swords and Deviltry, Swords against Death, Swords and Ice Magic, Rime Isle,* and *Bazaar of the Bizarre. Rime Isle* is a short novel included in the contents of *Swords and Ice Magic* without change of text.

Story Collections

Night's Black Agents. Sauk City, Wisconsin: Arkham House, 1947. Expanded edition. New York: Berkley, 1978.
The Mind Spider and Other Stories. New York: Ace Books, 1961.
Shadows with Eyes. New York: Ballantine, 1962.
Ships to the Stars. New York: Ace Books, 1964.
A Pail of Air. New York: Ballantine, 1964.
The Night of the Wolf. New York: Ballantine, 1966.
The Secret Songs. London: Rupert Hart-Davis, 1968.
Night Monsters. New York: Ace Books, 1969. Substantially different second version. London: Gollancz, 1974.
The Best of Fritz Leiber. Garden City, New York: Doubleday, Science Fiction Book Club edition, 1974; New York: Ballantine, 1974.
The Book of Fritz Leiber. New York: DAW Books, 1974.
The Second Book of Fritz Leiber. New York: DAW Books, 1975. These last two books were combined in hardcover with a new introduction as *The Book of Fritz Leiber, Volumes One and Two*, Boston: Gregg Press, G. K. Hall, 1980.
The Worlds of Fritz Leiber. New York: Ace Books, 1976.
Heroes and Horrors. Edited by Stuart David Schiff. Brown Mills, New Jersey: Whispers Press, 1978.
The Change War. Boston: Gregg Press, G. K. Hall, 1978.
The Ship of Shadows. London: Gollancz, 1979.

Poetry Collections

The Demons of the Upper Air. Glendale, California: Roy A. Squires, 1969.
Sonnets to Jonquil and All. Glendale, California: Roy A. Squires, 1978.

Edited by Fritz Leiber

The World Fantasy Awards, Vol. 2. Edited by Stuart David Schiff and Fritz Leiber. Garden City, New York: Doubleday, 1980. Includes a twenty-five-page Leiber essay about supernatural horror.

Short Pieces not Available in Leiber Collections

"Ervool." Short story printed as a limited edition chapbook, prepared for distribution at the Sixth World Fantasy Convention in Baltimore, Maryland, October, 1980. Roanoke, Virginia: Cheap Street, 1980. Includes a new Introduction by Leiber and an Afterword by Alva Rogers.

"The Pale Brown Thing." Two-part novella which was later revised and expanded for *Our Lady of Darkness. The Magazine of Fantasy and Science Fiction*. January and February, 1977.

"The Death of Princes." Short story reprinted in Carr, Terry, ed. *The Best Science Fiction of the Year, #6*. New York: Ballantine, 1977.

"A Rite of Spring." Short story reprinted in Carr, Terry, ed. *The Best Science Fiction of the Year #7*. New York: Ballantine, 1978.

"Black Glass." Short story reprinted in Carr, Terry, ed. *The Best Science Fiction of the Year, #8*. New York: Ballantine, 1979.

"Later Than You Think." Short story reprinted in Aldiss, Brian, ed. *Evil Earths*. New York: Avon, 1979.

"The Button Molder." Short story reprinted in Schiff, Stuart David, ed. *Whispers III*. Garden City, New York: Doubleday, 1981.

Nonfiction

Fantasy Books, regular book review column written by Leiber. Appeared in *Fantastic Stories* beginning with March, 1968 issue and ending in March, 1979. Column continued in *Locus* from that point forward, on an occasional basis.

On Fantasy, book review and criticism column by Leiber, appearing in alternating bimonthly issues of *Fantasy Newsletter* from 1980 forward.

"The Change War Series," Leiber's preface to story "No Great Magic." Pohl, Frederik, et al., eds. *The Great Science Fiction Series*. New York: Harper and Row, 1980.

"The Profession of Science Fiction: XII: Mysterious Islands." Essay by Leiber in *Foundation: The Review of Science Fiction*, 11 and 12. March, 1977.

"Travails of the Fantasy Novel: A Project Unborn." Essay by Leiber in *Foundation: The Review of Science Fiction*, 17. September, 1979.

Record Album

Fritz Leiber Reads Gonna Roll the Bones. Long-playing record album. AWR 3239. New York: Alternate World Recordings, 1977.

Selected Material About Fritz Leiber

Frane, Jeff. *Fritz Leiber. Starmont Reader's Guide: 8.* Mercer Island, Washington: Starmont, 1980. Sixty-four-page guide to Leiber's writings, with bibliography.

Garrett, Randall. *An Hour with Fritz Leiber.* Cassette recording. Hourglass Productions 10292.

Hills, Norman L. "Fritz Leiber." *Dictionary of Literary Biography,* vol. 8. Detroit: Gale Research Company, 1981.

———. "Fritz Leiber." *Twentieth Century Science Fiction Writers.* Edited by Curtis C. Smith. New York: Saint Martin's Press, 1981.

Leiber, Justin. "Fritz Leiber and Eyes." *Starship* (Summer 1979): 9–18.

Merril, Judith. "Fritz Leiber." *The Best from Fantasy and Science Fiction: A Special Twenty-Fifth Anniversary Anthology.* Edited by Edward L. Ferman. Garden City, New York: Doubleday, 1974. Includes bibliography.

Moskowitz, Sam. "Fritz Leiber." *Seekers of Tomorrow: Masters of Modern Science Fiction.* Cleveland and New York: World Publishing Company, 1966.

Purviance, Jim. "Algol Interview: Fritz Leiber." *Algol* (Summer-Fall 1978): 23–28.

Reginald, R., ed. "Fritz Leiber." *Science Fiction and Fantasy Literature,* vol. 2. Detroit: Gale Research Company, 1979.

Schweitzer, Darrell. "Fritz Leiber." *Science Fiction Voices #1.* San Bernardino, California: The Borgo Press, 1979.

Walker, Paul. "Fritz Leiber." *Speaking of Science Fiction.* Oradell, New Jersey: Luna Publications, 1978.

Index